Sockeye

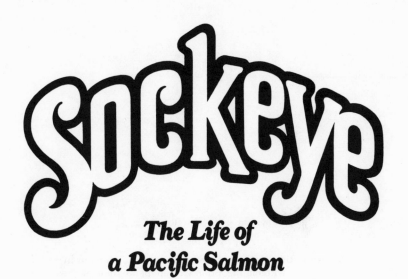

Sockeye

The Life of a Pacific Salmon

ROGER CARAS

The Dial Press
New York   1975

Manufactured in the United States of America

First printing, 1975

Library of Congress Cataloging in Publication Data

Caras, Roger A
    Sockeye.

      1. Sockeye salmon—Legends and stories.
I. Title.
QL795.F7C37   597′.55   75-22260
ISBN 0-8037-7247-5

This book is for Sy Reitknecht
who knew early and stayed long . . .

AUTHOR'S NOTE

This book is a continuation of a series that was begun in the early 1960s. Earlier volumes have dealt with the life histories of wolves, Kodiak bears, mountain lions and the California condor. Why now a book about a fish? When compared with the *personalities* of the other animals in this series a fish, even the salmon, hardly registers. Look at the dynamics of wolf society, the ponderous yet somehow graceful way in which the giant brown bear dominates in its habitat and the fantastic skill of the hunting cat. Even the condor, a primitive creature by avian standards, is a genius when compared with the sleekest and cleverest of fish.

A fish now because this is not a series or a book about animal intelligence, nor about what we usually like to project as animal personality. This is a book about survival and the ways in which animals have evolved for that paramount task. A wolf lives in wolf society not for the pleasure of it but because it is obviously the best way to go about things in the world where the wolf finds itself. The cat is a hunter not for the sport but so that it will not die of starvation. The ursine cycles of the year that are so peculiarly the bear's are all attuned to making it through for another round of breeding. The condor, fading now in history, almost forgotten by the thrust of avian evolution, also represents a success story engraved upon the annals of living matter. None of these animals surpasses the salmon, though, none is better at what it does than the salmon in its way. In the context of the stories we are trying to record, the salmon is perfect, the alternative to perfect in a hostile world, the next step down, in fact, being oblivion.

A fish is not the easiest animal to relate to. Communication is all but impossible for us and so are projection and comprehension. At night, by the fire, we can sit and listen to our dog whine in his sleep as his feet move in mock pursuit. The dog dreams and we wonder what his dreams can be like. A salmon doesn't dream, or at least so we believe. That is troublesome. How can one relate to an animal that cannot dream? The vertebrate animals we are in contact with most, mammals first and then birds, react to us. Mammals enjoy our touch, very often, and birds come to us in the barnyard or on their perch and we feed them. There is communion. With fish there is none. Not only do they not dream but even awake they refuse to acknowledge us. That is difficult for us, yet it is all the more reason why we should record the story we have here. Because they are so distant, so removed, so untouchable we could overlook the perfect natural genius of their survival. But if we are to truly belong to this planet as its dominant intellectual form, we must understand as much as we can. We must know as much about the salmon as we do about the American lion and the great wild dog. Each is a story of the perfection of being, the ultimate qualities always reflected in survival.

Sockeye

Chapter

1

It was before the great glaciers began their repeated crushing defeat of the Northern Hemisphere: the pre-Glacial
Epoch when the land and the water of the world did not
occupy their present areas, nor were they in the same
ratio. It was before the upheavals began when water
would be lifted from the sea by intensifying cold and laid
upon the land first as snow and then as ice, snow compact-
ing into ice from its own weight at a depth of twenty-eight
feet. The weight of the ice, lifted away from and dropping
the level of the sea, would later bear down onto the land
until it too would change level and place and sink deeper
into the waters that remained. That was to happen four
times, at least, but it was before then, much before, and it
was a different world. Animals that reigned then, largely,
are gone and man was coming but not yet here. His mighty
potential lay in the loins of creatures far less aware of self
and with fewer compulsions. Simpler animals suited
simpler times.

It was in those times which no true man ever saw (and
about which all men later and true would wonder), that

the genus *Salmo* found the passage across the North and ranged after fast-moving prey from the top of the Atlantic to the top of what would one day be known as the Pacific Ocean. To this genus the Atlantic salmon belonged and still do—and also the trout, fast, smart fish of stream and deep, secret and darkling pools.

In its primitive yet advancing world *Salmo* moved into depths and then up along coastal shelves, always feeding. They hunted and were hunted and moved with a rhythm we can never even guess. Their time and their rhythm are gone, for their fossil record is lost beneath a world even now frozen and crushed and unobtainable to our curiosity. We seek them in vain.

Then the ice ages began. Some land rose as the water fell and other land sank. Land and water changed places in a cosmic seesaw and animals died. Some *Salmo* stocks found themselves trapped as the land bridge between Asia and North America rose from beneath their very sea. The Bering Strait, the name by which we know it now, was closed and access to the Pacific was lost to the *Salmo*. Perhaps migrating animals and migrating men, in time, fed on the stocks of fish that boiled upward on the north bank of the new isthmus. The fish were answering a futile call to obey ancient ways. What windrows of dead and dying fish heaped high there and what the stench must have been like we can only guess, for we have no knowledge of numbers; but many *Salmo* fish must have perished. Some, though, survived. Of this we have evidence. New pressures were brought to bear on them as they piled up in a newly restricted world, but even these we cannot know or understand. It happened, we do not know how.

Under these indefinable pressures the fish evolved, perhaps rapidly as those things go, and soon *Salmo* gave way to new genera. Among them was *Oncorhynchus* and that genus, too, began to split and adapt and snatch every inch of opportunity away from a cold and dark world north of the land bridge. From that line came *kisutch* the coho and *tshawytscha* the chinook, *keta* the chum and *gorbuscha* the pink salmon. It was there that the first seeds of *Nerka* the sockeye appeared. It is of the sockeye we speak here— *Oncorhynchus nerka,* down from *Salmo,* down from fish of another ocean, down from time and unknowable history, and invisible relics lost in land that was, and was not, and was again time over time in speculative sequences that taunt us. From there *Nerka* came to write its history upon the Pacific world and never again to taste the saline Atlantic or compete there in that arena for survival. Its back turned on the lost and forgotten, it exploded toward the West, creating a vibrant, living bridge between Asia and North America.

The order in which these species evolved is again largely speculative. Some formed in part at least, we believe, north of the land bridge, before it sank again beneath melting snow and ice that returned the oceans to their former beaches. Perhaps some waited until the land fell back into the sea and life to the north could pour southward, swirl in great eddies as pools on the north rim opened and spilled into corresponding cuts in the beach to the south. Long before the bridge was fully gone from sight, even as the water rose an inch at a time, year after year, fish beat across the narrowing ridge pulled away to the south by the magnitude of the Pacific and the power of most ancient memories. The migratory routes were probably not the same but the lure was, the memory was, the tug that drew them flopping across the land and into a remembered sea. With all the rest *Nerka* was there and this fish, the sockeye, too, had to find a way of blending memory and new evolutionary gains into a pattern that would spell survival. For behind it all, behind the wind-rows along the beaches, beyond the heaps of stinking fishwreck and behind the pools that filled and overflowed and suffocated because they did not keep their promise and open to the sea, behind all this wild surging was the single powerful will to survive.

The sockeye, like its *Salmo* ancestors, was anadromous. That had not been lost. As a salmon it would always breed in sweet waters above the sea and then return to the sea at some point to mature. At that juncture, in its time of ripe-ness, it would again ascend its own river, its own stream and seek its natal gravel bed to breed. But a change had occurred, a strange and deadly adaptation. Whereas the Atlantic salmon could return year after year to their stream and reproduce before heading down again into the sea, those that thrust southward into the Pacific as *On-corhynchus* could not. They would ascend but once, for the Pacific salmon die after thrashing through a single re-productive cycle. It was a change, a strange alteration of a much more ancient system; but in time, it would be shown, this too would work. The seas and the rivers that emptied into them, the smaller streams and the lakes beyond filled with fish. By the scores of billions they were hatched and died and more billions of birds and mammals and other fish fed upon them. Newly down from an older line, they fitted into a place and a scheme and a pattern that spelled life, life in the Pacific and its periphery. That was unchanged. Patterns change and styles, places and conditions, but there remains that single constant—life and the will to live on as a species and an individual, the last perhaps less compelling than the first. And so, in the Pacific world, there was the sockeye, a product of time and force and the forward movement of all things.

Chapter

2

Many stages had to pass, first in the gravel bed of the feeder stream above the lake, then in the lake, and then below it as it ran away from the hills and mountains to the sea. As an alevin, young *Nerka* had hatched from its egg with a yolk sac attached to its underside. A month after it had been deposited in the gravel as an egg, an eye had begun to show. It was a time of mortality, for life was tender and the threads were thin on which it hung. But *Nerka* had survived, and—subjected to water whose temperature, flow and chemistry had remained within critical bounds—the time of hatching had finally come. Far too vulnerable, yet, to venture forth into the flowing water beyond the gravel-bound pockets, it remained hidden, holding back while absorbing a chemical memory.

Hour by hour the alevin grew, its sex was differentiated; it would one day be a male. But that was years away. Now *Nerka* had to grow and, above all, survive. As the future salmon grew, its yolk sac diminished, was used each minute, each hour. It contained a perfectly balanced diet of proteins, carbohydrates, minerals and vitamins. A great blood vessel ran through the center of the sac, the vitelline vein. Through its permeable walls the alevin obtained its oxygen. And that gas fed the flame of its life.

The transition from egg to alevin had occurred for *Nerka* in February. All around, in the tiny pockets formed between grains of gravel other eggs were opening to allow other infant fish to emerge into the stream above the lake. Flakes and chips of former mountains and other ages that had rolled and tumbled across a harsh and rocky river bottom until their size was right now formed a nursery for future tenants of the sea. The exquisite interrelationships here, beyond the minds of men, made life possible. The nature of the mountain, thrust up from a prior sea, the nature of those rocks, their hardness, their ability to fracture and then be rounded in the tumbling of melting snow and ice—these factors made life for the salmon possible, for there had to be just enough room for each alevin to hover and absorb that which was hatched as a part of itself. And water had to reach each creature, flow over and around it and imprint it with a memory that would help guide its recall from the sea at maturity.

There was near-total protection from predators for the infants from the hatching in the second month of the year until the next phase of their life began in the fifth and for some the sixth. Occasionally an accident would occur. A wading bear, rude and oblivious, would upset some gravel where its huge paws fell crashing through the surface of the stream and occasionally other animals would dig in the gravel for a treasure and some alevins would be cast out of their pockets into the flow of the stream lakeward bound. There would be no dirges sounded for these creatures untimely cast, but they would die. Unable to counter current or fend or resist predation, torn from their sacs as they were tumbled across the roofs where other alevins hid in safety below, they dissolved back into the world of water from which their substance had been originally borrowed. Aborted, torn and consumed, they vanished, but their number was few. Most alevins, in fact, become yolk-attached, and, both fed and washed by the elements of the superb master plan, survive.

But, May and June are different kinds of months for the salmon-to-be, and the alevins in those pre- and early summer days lose their yolk sacs. One day, having shrunk into near-nothingness, the last of the good, the last of the egg material is gone and the alevin are no longer called by that name. They have become fry. One at a time and then in small eddies they emerge from the gravel. They nose up and push free and enter the stream as both prey and predator. The fry hunt, they seek plankton and even the smaller insects. Microscopic life they seek as microscopic life they very nearly were in the weeks just past.

All manner of fish and other water predators seek the fry; it is a time of great attrition. Many die from each hatching. Free-swimming, though, and filled with the incredible will to survive, they learn to dodge and avoid and escape. They turn downstream and move with the current. They do not linger long in the stream above the lake but seek the lake itself.

It is here that the sockeye salmon distinguishes itself from the rest of its Pacific salmon kin. The fry of the pink and the chum, many emerging in the same and sister streams just below the lake, move directly down current and into the sea. Their time in sweet water once they emerge as fry can be numbered in days. The sockeye fry, though, hang back from the sea for years. From fry the sockeye grow to be parr, or fingerlings as they are sometimes known, and from parr or fingerlings to smolt. As smolt they are ready for the final descent into the sea.

The original sockeye eggs from which the alevin emerged had been pink, bright pink, and they had been protected from the sun in their gravel pockets. The alevin had been pink as well, but as fry they began the transition to tarnished silver for their residence in the lake. From area to area that may vary, but the thrust of the color change is toward the tone of an old, hard-used and pocket-tossed coin.

As the youngest of the true juveniles, and vulnerable to hazards beyond reasonable measure, the fry move quickly into the lake guided, we think, by current but perhaps by tug and pull we have not yet guessed. The water of the lake, quieter, deeper, stiller, has a different taste, a different smell, a different ambient quality; these and perhaps other things trigger the newest patterns. For the salmon, products of a shallow and gravel-bedded stream, even the shallows of the lake are deep, and the fry move alone really but seemingly in bunches toward every scrap of cover that reveals itself to them. A log moved into the lake by melting snow that has grown sodden enough to sink becomes shelter for hundreds; reeds and other bottom growth serve for thousands more. Perhaps stunned, momentarily slowed by the new experience, the kindergarten fish seek first cover and then the dimensions of their newest world. But first there is the instinct for cover.

The fry enter a dynamic community of fish; by no means is the lake their own. In the shallowest waters that they first explore are peamouth, redside shiner, lake chub, dace both leopard and longnose, a kind of carp, argumentative and ferociously territorial little three-spine sticklebacks and at least two forms of sculpin. As they move into deeper water there are lake trout, burbot, whitefish and suckers of several kinds. Later, in open areas of the lake there will be others, some of them dangerous—cutthroat trout and rainbows, the char or Dolly Varden, coho salmon, kokanee and squawfish. All of these are neighbors in the lake and not all neighbors of little fish are to be trusted. Some are sluggish, slow and graze upon their world in leisure time. Others are slicers and slashers of water, swift-darting shadowing forms that pass a spot like a blade, swooping away with other life half consumed before their presence is suspected. No fish in the lake to which *Nerka* descended, no other creature either, none would be capable of mercy or regard. Each sockeye fry descends to the lake as living protein and each is fair game for all. In the world of the eaters and the eaten there are no rules except manage the one and avoid the other. There is no plea uttered and none heard. Each creature lives or dies upon the whim of chance so complex and so seemingly indiscriminate that description and interpretation both fail. This was the new world for *Nerka*, the first step down from the natal stream, the first rung down to the sea.

Chapter

3

Nerka would have two years in the lake. Entering as a fry, he would leave and go down to the sea with the second May freshet as a fingerling smolt. In the sea he would grow to be a blue-tinged silver fish of speed and stamina. His kind is the slimmest and most streamlined of all the salmon species. So perfect are they at what they do it is moot whether they were made for the sea, or the sea for them.

The lake itself is above Cook Inlet north and east of the Alaskan Peninsula. It is north, too, of the fabled Kodiak Archipelago. Its name is Coppertree, and the river that emptied into it above and flows away to the sea below is called Coppertree Creek. No one knows where the name comes from. The lake is nestled in an area of alder and birch, of evergreens that finger the sky and then suddenly relinquish the land to areas of scrub. There are blueberry patches, and they plus the guaranteed salmon run every year make it a paradise for bears. There are brown bear in the vicinity for most of the year, gruff shuffling giants, rude and coarse; and there are moose and fox, of course, fox after the leavings of the sloppy bears. There are black bear, cinnamon and black, actually, but generically black, and there are wolf and deer. The smaller animals, weasels to voles, number in the tens of thousands around the Coppertree's perimeter and along the banks of its river. Osprey fish; the northern race of bald eagle fishes, too, and also plays the scavenger taking whatever is to be had. Ravens, crows, nutcrackers, jays and magpies vie to outdo each other in rudeness; lesser birds come and go with the season. The sunlit hours ride a wide-swinging pendulum and the lesser birds, the smaller perchers, are dictated to by seasons' march and respond in order to survive. Coppertree is south of the Arctic yet north of the temperate surprise of southeastern Alaska. It is an almost-world, a place of fog and rain and then sudden balmy calm. Harsh and cruel, gentle and caressing, the world of the Coppertree does what it wishes and its schedule of events is its own. As sodden as the forest and the sky might ever be as they hang above the Coppertree, the salmon fry are restricted forever to the world beneath the surface of the lake and the river systems that support it or are sustained by it. Occasionally, in the final frenzy of their spawning run, the hen and cocks might thrust across a spit of land, a forgotten intrusion of sand and gravel. But for almost every moment of their life they live in the more temperate and temporizing world submerged.

In order to survive this next great phase in his life, *Nerka* had to enter Coppertree Lake at a time that coincided with several phenomena. There would be enough tricks of chance in his time as it was without allowing basic rhythms to run high risks as well. Those had to pulse with the planet, with the weather enveloping all and with the beat and march of other forms of life.

SOCKEYE

The first coincidence was that *Nerka* as a fry had to enter the lake at a time when the ice was breaking up for it was then that optimum conditions of temperature, oxygen, and prey were available. The top yard of water had been brick-hard for months, but as May approached it grew thinner by the day. Water from the uplake Coppertree Creek flowed across the warming surface and pockets and dents began to form and then collapse inward. Sheets of ice deteriorated into spines and spicules and these, too, became frayed by the eroding warmth of earth-tilt and time-change. Each day was longer than the one before and each promised more sun to follow. The color patterns that flowed across the fracturing world of ice were at places in the spectrum for which words have not yet been invented. Rain, when it fell, came through a warmer sky and chewed at the lake's icelock and fragmented it until hunks broke loose and began to find the downlake river flow sloughing away at the edges as they went. Winds came and went, ice blocks rocked and pushed and their rudeness further eroded the hold of a winter gone and dead. And then the lake was free. The Alaskan months of chill and harshness had come and gone again, bringing life and death in equal shares. The animals that now came down to the lake to drink were the best of their kind and they carried the genes of the future. The birds that now worried over nesting site with song and posture were also the better of their species and they, too, were bridges from the past to the future, the bearers of genes and promise and evolving wonder.

The second coincidence of *Nerka*'s coming to the Coppertree Lake was the proliferation of life there. Day by day the plankton population was increasing for it was spring beneath the surface as well as above. Small crustaceans, small enough for the fry to eat, swam in profusion and were there to build the ounces of salmon flesh. The insects that spend their infant stages on the lake bottom and in its middle waters were there, too, by the billion and *Nerka*, as he grew, could rise to the surface where aerial insects would sometimes fall and pock the surface. They could be pulled below and used as well. The planktonic crustacea, though, copepods and the cladocerans like Daphnia and Bosminia, constituted *Nerka*'s staple diet.

It was a time when the level of the lake rose and spilled out across its own grassy banks. Ice and snow further up the system rushed down the creek, swelling it and carrying the fry to the waiting lake below even as they swelled the lake itself. For a time, during those first days, *Nerka* moved among the blades of grass that would soon, in the summer months, be land again. Where deer would brose *Nerka* now hunted. Where grouse would wander and strut *Nerka* prowled, an infant seeking to eat other infants. Other fish prowled there, too, and only infinitely unfathomable luck of numbers allowed this fry to survive. He was one of millions that would live, of course, around the entire northern Pacific periphery, but billions of others died. Trout and carp and other creatures that share the lakes and rivers with the sockeye fry seek to build their flesh too, for it is their spring as well. *Nerka* darted for prey and darted equally often for shelter. The future land grass was useful, it provided cover almost as thick as the redd in which the egg had become an alevin even before it had become a fry.

Once the fry have taken up their truly pelagic existence they do not distribute themselves equally throughout the world of the lake. Although in the winter months they will sink away from the ice and seek deeper mild waters and basin hollows, in their first spring and summer they remain close to the surface. They live as part of an enormously complex limnological community and circulate with it. Masses of planktonic crustacea circulate slowly with currents within the lake's boundaries and the young fry stay with the moving, undulating feast. In the darker hours of day, early morning, late afternoon and days of hard rain and lowering skies, the fry rise to within a foot or two of the surface and at times come all the way to the surface itself. When the sun is highest and the summer most nearly keeping pace with promise, the fry circulate with their banquet from fifteen to twenty feet down. The edges of these masses of life are frayed, of course, individuals and small clusters drift up and down and away, but this is the general pattern. It is less casual than it may seem for the needs of all species are met.

Instinctively each sockeye fry in the lake concentrates on eating. The larger it grows, the more quickly it achieves fingerling size and the larger the fingerling it becomes, the better its chances for survival. In the early pelagic days of May, the fry each consume three-tenths of a milligram of food a day. By midsummer that rises to over thirty-one milligrams each twenty-four hours, and although the winter sees the figure reduced sharply as food supplies dwindle, April of the following year will see the individual needs reach toward forty milligrams between sunrise and sunrise. The population of the Cyclops and Daphnia, the Epischura and Bosminia in the lake explode to meet the challenge. Like the Cosmos with its uncountable billions of units of light, the minute crustacea expand geometrically and *Nerka* was to feed along with the rest. He survived his weeks in the redd as egg and alevin, he challenged the uplake river reach as a fry and then rode the current to the lake with the ice breakup in springtime thaw. He skirted danger on gravel bed and among weeds and reeds never known to him before. Sunken objects held safety and peril in equal share. He learned to dart and duck and feed while avoiding hazards that grew by the minute.

Nerka now was part of a perfect circle and at any moment he could be plucked away to dissolve as the food of something else. His mission was clear. He was entered in the race to see if he could survive long enough to pass across a redd near the one where he was hatched. He was to live long enough to spread his seed across the gravel and the unfertilized eggs that had begun to settle there. Then his fate didn't matter. Chemistry is a leisurely element in life to which all must come back in the end, so never is there any kind of rush. It is what comes before the chemical return that matters and that was the cycle into which fate had decreed *Nerka* must enter. A future male salmon, he was a spark of life in a spark-filled world. Other sparks filled eagles and bears, others birds and men. Whales, too, are sparks and all that are smaller than that. The sparks is the life and the purpose, the chemistry the framework that holds it all and in the end collects it all, all but the spark and that—the destiny of the spark—is the greatest mystery there is.

Chapter

4

Even as *Nerka* pushed forward through each day toward his destiny, his private history was being written thousands of times, repeated over and over on each scale of his body. If eyes of man were ever to examine this single fish, the days of his life could be read.

Throughout his years circuli or sclerites were laid on his scales until they gave the appearance of ridges. Under a microscope they would be as clear as the growth rings of a tree. In summer, when his growth would be rapid because of the abundance of food, the circuli would be far apart, widely separated as his growth increased. In winter, when his rate of growth would slow, the markings would be closer together. They are known to men as winter bands and their count is the recorded age of the fish. When he finally moved down through the last rung of the sweet water system where he was hatched, *Nerka* would then be plunging ahead toward maturity. The circuli would be less delicate and their grosser nature would be easy to see. A knowing eye could tell the seasons in the lake from the seasons in the sea. If he was to be an average fish, his years would number between two and seven. The time allowed for the full and miraculous life of his spark was no more than that—and no more was needed. All that a salmon is or can be is locked in step with the lives and styles of the other creatures with whom *Nerka* would have contact. The meshing meant that all would survive, all species at least, and despite appearances there was no capriciousness. It was locked, fixed, productive and whole— chemistry taken from an inanimate system and made alive for a while. In the end all would meet an inevitable common fate with the stuff of their life returning for use again. We know of no perfection beyond this, and nothing more miraculous.

As the young salmon moved out into the lake, as he became a viable element in the world of the Coppertree, his survival would depend in large part upon his ability to react; and in order to react he had to receive signals. Although his brain was small, too small and too simple to allow for much learning, it was superbly attuned to the senses which in turn were exquisitely receptive to all that went on around him. His eyes, for example, were remarkably like those of man although water is a far different medium, a far poorer conductor of light than air.

Nerka's eye was a camera. Light rays entered through the lens at the transparent center of the eyeball. From there they were directed with precision onto a light-sensitive screen, the retina. Where the human eye has an iris or diaphragm in front of the lens to control the light coming through, *Nerka's* eye had none. The iris was fixed. But there was no loss of control. A perfect system had otherwise been evolved. In the screen or retina at the rear of his eye there were two kinds of receptor cells—rods and cones—and each sent their messages to his brain. The cone cells could receive color and were at least thirty times as sensitive as the rods, black-and-white receptors only. During the day, when the sun played across the lake's surface, the cone cells were in use; but as the light level fell, as evening crept in across the surrounding hills and fingers of dark slipped in between the trees, then a miraculous thing would occur. The cone cells that had been active since dawn would begin an actual retreat, back into the deeper and darker layers of the retina, while the rod-shaped cells moved forward. During the bright hours of the day the rods remained hidden in that same deeper and darker tissue, protected against the light that could injure them.

Nerka was nearsighted, for nowhere would he ever be where visibility would come close to equaling the world above the surface. In the most crystalline water 99 per cent of the light is lost at twenty-seven feet. When storm toss and high river flow create regions of murk, little light can penetrate beyond a dozen feet. The plankton fields upon which *Nerka* grazed further reduced the light available to him and his visibility range ran from five to a true optimum of forty feet. In fact the food that *Nerka* hunted, the minute crustaceans and insect larvae, acted on him as fog and smoke does on the vision of man. They blocked and scattered the light coming toward him in the water. If his world had been perceived visually alone, it would have been confusing and even more rich in hazard. As it was, his visual judgment of his world was based on two phenomena, movement and contrast. A flash, a movement, a change of light values, a shadow, a silvery belly, these made the visual quality of *Nerka*'s world subject to interpretation. Without them it would have evened out into a foggy sameness beyond his discerning, beyond his reading.

There was another strange aspect to *Nerka*'s visual

world. It was the sameness of it, the constancy of cold
light. Fish do see color, of that there can be no doubt, but
water is cruel to red. The red-yellow-orange range, the
warm end of the spectrum, disappears almost as soon as a
light ray penetrates the surface, and what do manage to
sink deepest are green and blue.

On calm days when *Nerka's* body was oriented upward,
the underside of the Coppertree's surface was a silver mirror, and when the water was shallow even a reflection of
the bottom might play there. There was this silver and the
silver signals of other moving fish, but even silver is cold.
That was the world he saw and the only world he could
ever see—fractured light, bouncing light, refracted streams
and jets of silvery blue and greenish-silver in a world of
constant motion. It was a cold world of cold light and it
was for this that both *Nerka* and his eyes had been fash-
ioned.

Nerka was far more dependent on his sense of smell
than man can ever understand. Unlike his counterparts on
the land his nostrils did not connect with his throat. Instead, each ended in a chamber lined with sensing cells so
utterly fine we seek in vain for a valid comparison. Over
half a million receptors per square inch interpreted the
minute chemical messages that were pulsed inward by
fine cilia. They moved in rhythm to assure the constant
flow of information into these chambers and from there to
the brain. Indeed, man has always wondered over the in-
disputable fact that the largest part of the fish's brain is
given over to this single task, the interpretation of and re-
action to the sense of smell. *Nerka* could detect traces of
gas and more solid matter far beyond our detection. Like a
finely tuned instrument, he locked his visual world and his
chemical world together and used them in tandem to hunt
and to successfully elude hunters.

SOCKEYE

From the moment he emerged from his pink egg as a pink alevin—perhaps before that, for all we know—*Nerka* had another use for his sense of smell as well. Perhaps his use of this sense is greater than that of any other animal on earth, or at least so some people believe. He began at once developing a chemical memory. He began a process of imprinting so beyond comprehension that we sometimes long to deny it on that basis alone, its strangeness to us. When *Nerka* left the Coppertree and migrated through its lower reaches to the sea, he would program his memory to unwind again with incredible precision. No matter how many thousands of miles he might wander during his sea-years of growth, this memory would one day at least in part help him to smell his way home again and do that well enough to rest at last over the gravel bed where he had been spawned and hatched. For *Nerka*, resident of what to us is the utter sameness of the water world, no watery place, no liquid track smelled the same as any other. And his brain, that brain we call small, could remember the infinite details that built that fact with shreds of scent. Try as we will, we can never really understand how that is done. If we could record with the same precision and permanence the product of our sensory intrusions as what *Nerka* learned from his streams and his lake and what he would later learn in the avenues and alleys of the sea, what manner of intellect would we be? But we think, we conjure, we calculate and we learn, and so we cannot spare the proportion of brain *Nerka* could devote to this aspect of his salmon existence.

There was more. *Nerka*'s sense of hearing was no less stunning. His ears were buried deep inside his head and were not exposed to the water at all. There were no flaps, no holes and no eardrums as we understand them. Sounds conveyed to him in a turbid and even polluted world could be interpreted as they passed through his skin, his flesh and his bone to reach the ears safely placed away from trauma. Miraculously he was able to distinguish the good from the bad. All his life, as if by magic, he would be able to tell the sounds of those that hunted him from those of the creatures which he had to hunt in order to live. And all of this came with him in the egg. He learned practically none of it himself. It had been learned for him.

And yet even this was not enough. *Nerka*'s hearing was enhanced to an incredible degree by tiny pods strung out along the length of his body. These cupolas were lined with sensory hairs and connected by tubes to the surface of his skin in two lines running the length of his body from his head to his tail. Called lateral lines, they enabled him to detect even the lowest frequencies. The tiny canals picked up the lowest thudding disturbance, and when the information of that was coupled with the actual sense of hearing, *Nerka*'s ability to pinpoint source was beyond anything we can ever even approximate. Up to thirty feet away *Nerka*, stationary and attentive, could read the sounds of his world. Beyond that his lateral lines would fail him; and dependent on inner, hidden ear alone, he would have to swim a search pattern.

As *Nerka* reacted to the world around him, he often did so in a rippling sensory pattern. Either sound or smell might first attract him to prey or danger, and one or the other might at first predominate in worth. The one, though, would soon overlap and play off the other until sight became of value. Then, with sight, smell and sound in harmony the fish could become a truly responsive mechanism. Another chemical-reception system, taste, also helped him monitor his world. Unlike man, his taste buds were not limited to the interior of his mouth. They occurred as well on his lips and snout. He could taste something by simply brushing it and need never endanger himself by ingesting something he could detect as bad.

Man has long wondered how well fish can feel, respond to texture and immediate pressure. This is not yet measurable by means we know, but we assume that it is reasonably acute. It worked well enough for *Nerka,* and by this means, too, he judged his world and used it more quickly than he would allow himself to be used by it. One touch we know was sure and swift in value. *Nerka* could judge temperature and even navigate by it. He could follow beacons of heat and cold, currents that led to and from where he chose to be or not to be. Ribbons of temperature ran through his world, a warp against the woof of silvery green and blue, against the texture of sound and pressure sensed along the length of his body and against the fabric of smell and taste. He used it all without knowing and without the ability to care. It was there in the egg, it was there while he busied himself with his yolk sac content, and it was there as he grew. It would always be with him. He was a spark and these senses were the contents of that flaring, flashing miracle of life. All of it would die with him. All would dull and fade as his life faded; but that was later, after the lake, after the sea.

Chapter

5

Nerka's life was one of movement. He swam to get from one place to another; when in currents and eddies, he swam to stay in place. He moved both toward food and away from peril. He was designed, totally, every part of him, to move through a medium many times the density of air. Unlike the surface animals of the land, very much like the birds in this one regard, he lived a life that was as vertically oriented as it was horizontal. He moved forward no more often and no less than he did up and down.

As a mature cock *Nerka* would be able to explode forward at fourteen miles an hour. He would not be able to sustain such a speed, but he would be capable of achieving it. As a fry he could come nowhere close to that, but he was still, in miniature, the swimming animal he would always be. His coordination was as smooth as the passage of a season and as true to set form. In a forward movement, either in pursuit of a minute animal or as an escape tactic, he would go from a stretched-out streamlined form into a virtual semicircle in less than one-thirtieth of a second. Stroking hard he could arc his body until the same maximum curvature was achieved in the opposite direction and that in less than one-twentieth of a second. His velocity now close to maximum, he could repeat the stroke again in one-thirtieth of a second and then glide with his body extended. This could be repeated as often as needed. It was too swift properly to be seen, but the results were clear.

As he moved through the water, he created his own complex pattern of eddies. Upstream falls and rapids were no more dynamic than these, and no more complicated. The fact that they were in miniature simply suited the scale of the animal himself. As he grew, the currents and eddies he would create with each move would increase and blend in with the billions of others created by all the other creatures in the lake or the sea. No one has ever reckoned the role of these in the movements of the Cosmos, how such energy blends with all others so released and how they play upon each other. This much is certain, though: with his exquisite sensory equipment *Nerka* could read those currents created by the creatures around him and judge their worth, judge their peril. Even as he created currents and sent water particles swirling against each other and in concert against other forms of life, he interpreted second by second those that returned to him from other sources. As he moved with other fish, they communicated by the gentle pressures that the movement of each exerted on all others. When we think of the fish, we must think of this, the degree to which it is locked in step with the Cosmos as well as with smaller wonders. It is all one, and *Nerka* a part of it.

By the time *Nerka* was ready to go to sea, 96 per cent of the young produced in the spawning run of his parents would be dead. Many of them would die in the lake, in that two-season residence in sweet water above the sea. A principal and deadly foe of all salmon fry is the Dolly Varden char. A fast and greedy fish, it seeks the sockeye fry and at any one time may have as many as ninety of the infants in its stomach, ninety of that year's crop.

Nerka had fed well on a passing raft of crustaceans, a planktonic feast circling the edge of a lake basin with an easy current. The current was born in the creek above the lake, born where *Nerka* had been spawned, and it blended with others coming in above and below the lake. It drifted around in lazy circle and carried flotsam with it. Occasionally small treasures would be snatched from it by countering currents and intersecting eddies, but most of what it claimed traveled with it, round and round. *Nerka* had joined it as he often did and drifted in among the motes that sparkled and caught and kicked free cool silver-green light. Bubbles drifted among the motes and these were gems, too, gems that hung and glittered mid-water. *Nerka* browsed on the eternal feast and tasted and felt and sensed as much as he could of his ambient world. He was growing and that was the present mission. Now he competed for food with others, not always his own kind.

As he dropped back from the drifting cloud of crustacean prey he slowly let himself down deeper, behind a sodden tree, to where some weeds grew in small clusters. The water was no more than a tall man deep there and the sun splashed down above, bright and yellow against the Coppertree world. A slight breeze blew and chopped the surface and broke its mirror. Through the fractured shards of water the light fell and came glistening against the pebbles and the boulders toward which *Nerka* sank. It was an hour when the water was full of jewels and the bottom sparkled like a pirate's chest of booty newly opened to the sun.

Then, suddenly, there were signals. *Nerka* turned to

find their source, to seek the meaning. His interpreting of them had to be almost instantaneous or his life could end. It generally was that swift.

A greedy Dolly Varden char had drifted in with a small bottom eddy and hung among the weeds only feet away. It had fed all day and killed three-score sockeye fry. Hunger was less the motivation than habit. It had been eating and would continue to eat until an unknown calling prompted it to drift away toward a deep place to digest the lives it had ended. Suddenly it, too, sensed the encounter. As fine a creature as *Nerka* was, he sent signals that others could discern. Even as he was sensed, *Nerka* sensed the Dolly Varden turn toward him amid the weeds and make the first tentative flick of its tail. The large and powerful body started forward in a first glide. In a second or less it would lash once and as designed would be in full pursuit. Mouth open, greedy jaws apart, it would strike and gulp at once and *Nerka* would vanish like all the rest. No chewing, no biting, just a single gulping motion, an opening and a closing, one cycle and all that *Nerka* was or promised to be would be over.

But *Nerka* had been well supplied. All the traits and powers destined to the sockeye breed were in him. At the first tail movement a wave of warning struck his side and slid along the microscopic tube endings from head to tail. The canals opened and the sensory cells read true. There was no need for *Nerka* to understand or linger on the signals; they bypassed such wasteful measures. *Nerka* moved, too. Just as the human hand releases a hot poker before the human brain can think of heat, so the fry reacted before any other process could occur. The Dolly Varden char passed on its profitless search and *Nerka* hovered low near where a boulder overhung a shiny place full

of dancing chips of sun. It was the kind of darting existence the salmon would live for two years in the lake. At
each stage of his life and growth there would be different
fish offering the greater threat, but there was no day, no
night when this evasive action would not be required
scores of times. By rote, without powers of thought, without knowledge of fear in any form we can understand, but
by merely being, he learned the safe places, and there he
hung and lingered as often as possible. When necessary he
ventured forth and drifted with mists of food, always dropping back toward shelter whenever sated. It was during
his rise toward food and fall away from it that he was most
vulnerable. Still, somehow, *Nerka* lived on. Each day his
promise increased, for each day he grew and came closer
to that day when he would be a cock salmon needed by the
Coppertree above the lake where it could all begin again.

Chapter

6

And so that first summer passed into fall. *Nerka* was progressing rapidly through his fry stage and could be properly called either a fingerling or a parr, the former perhaps more nearly correct since he was a fish of a Pacific species.

It had been a time of growth and of honing. He had become larger and faster although still minute and vulnerable as the community of the lake was viewed. All around him fish spawned at the same time and even by the same female and fertilized by the same male had died. Some had been infested with minute parasites and so slowed in their reflexes that they were the more easily taken. Others had fallen prey to fast trout and greedy Dolly Varden through no fault or weakness other than that to which all living creatures are subjected—chance and perhaps piscine fate. Still, enough, as always, had lived and among them was *Nerka*. He was a complete fish, full of those things that made his kind a species, different from all other kinds. He had passed the seemingly impossible test of a single spring and a single summer; now a fall and a winter lay ahead.

SOCKEYE

The avenues that run from the Coppertree system to the Arctic are broad and open. Cold pours down like a fluid substance. One day summer is gone and leaves are turning and falling. Branches of green become red, or yellow, and then they are brown and then they are bare. Small, tightly furled buds contain the assurance of another year, but for a season it is over.

The cold ache from the North that fell across the land caused radical changes in the lake as well. Water can remain liquid for only a brief band of the heat spectrum— from 32 to 212 degrees Fahrenheit. Above that it is steam and below it is ice. And it was ice that began to exert its force upon the world of the fry, ice that had always been there as one of water's amazing potentials.

Water, as a liquid, consists of a double molecule, dihydrol. When it becomes ice it is triple in form and is called trihydrol. Even water contains some trihydrol, though, and as its temperature drops the percentage of those molecules increases. At first these triple molecules with all the threat they hold are in solution, but as the air above cools and sucks heat from the water body, the density of that solution increases. At freezing point the triple molecules precipitate and an almost-solid exists where once there was a liquid.

The first ice was not crystalline, but appeared as small disklike particles. They were, in fact, neither liquid nor truly a solid yet, rather a colloid, the mysterious in-between state of matter. The colloid particles grew rapidly as the air temperature dropped. Snow was falling and flakes were dying on the surface of the water. In hours they would be able to accumulate there. Below, the fish retreated.

In the water another intermediate phase came and passed. The ice was half-colloid and half-solid and then, almost suddenly, it was crystalline. The Coppertree had begun to freeze over. There was a buoyant mass, cloudy, less subject to agitation than water itself, and it floated more than half submerged. A sodden, as yet insecure mass shut the lake away from the sky.

Near the intake from the Coppertree stream above the lake the ice acted like soggy canvas, rising and falling and sighing with the current. Toward the center of the lake the weight of it quieted the effects of the wind. A better conductor of heat than either water or snow, it yet provided a protective blanket over the lake. It was far colder above than below. Snow falling more rapidly with each hour lay across the ice, caught the wind and bunched against itself and added to the protective layer. A billion times a billion essentially hexagonal patterns with their beauty lost and forgotten in the very mass of the fall added a quietness to the world. Sounds were absorbed and only the wind and the occasional crack of a breaking limb were heard. But the harmonics were gone, just hard, initial sounds. Snow cleans everything on first fall, ground, air and sound. Below there was just the hiss of the water and the miniature sounds far beneath our range, but critical in the life of a salmon fry. The light level, of course, fell and *Nerka* sank toward deeper places yet.

Above, far beyond *Nerka*'s world but interacting with it as all forces on earth play upon another, falling snow passed through a mass of yet unfrozen water droplets. The crystals picked up a coating of rime and fell to the lake's newly solid surface as tapioca snow. A fog, a sudden and short-lived product of a pocket of warmer air, blew across the lake and the shores and froze midair. Ice needles formed and trees and shrubs took on the familiar look of winter fairy dust.

It was a world transformed. A dropping temperature

catching a world of land and water unprepared played trick upon trick, and within thirty-six hours one world gave way to another, another logically next in line. Animals died in those first hours of the Alaskan winter, birds and mammals both. They were the least of their kind or at least the most unlucky. Others survived and steeled themselves against what their instincts knew better than they would come. Those animals equipped to avoid the winter scene quickly adjusted. Grunting bears went to ground with little grace on the north-facing slopes of available hills, the better to be snowed in and protected. Squirrels went to their trees and barely bothered to scold each other, aching as they were with the sudden winter hurt.

Below, *Nerka*'s kind was not unaffected. There was mortality again. Each phase of the salmon's life is designed, apparently, to cull, to clip, to remove those fish furthest from perfection. And fish of other kinds, too, rose to float and bob against the rough underside of the new ice of spicule and needle and rime.

Nerka sank deeper. Adjusting, as he had since the time of his spawning, he automatically sought ways to survive the new and unfamiliar forces. The light was different, the water was different; he had come to a different place. Nevertheless, even as hunters were leaving fresh first tracks in the snow beside the lake the hunters in the lake, too, were aprowl. *Nerka* settled in some weeds near where others of his kind had also instinctively come and within inches of where he hovered for the moment a trout struck. It was a slashing, a twisting, a sliding past and when the trout was gone another four salmon had died. *Nerka* felt nothing for them, for he felt nothing for himself. Unaware of self, aware of neither life nor death—except how to live the one and avoid the other—he could be involved with nothing that could have even the most rudimentary suggestion of emotion. In the presence of death he knew only to move away.

The food supply in the weeks that followed dwindled but did not vanish. There was enough freely available protein in the lake so that *Nerka* and those others destined to see the ocean in following years could survive. It was a time of diminished growth, a time when the striations on the scales of fish grow smaller, finer and form the clear winter bands. It was winter, a holding time, a time to be seen through, for it held no reward and no promise save that which would surely follow. In a swinging pendulum this was the least time, the slowest time, and in the deep of the lake neither more nor less hazardous than better days. *Nerka*, next to be a smolt, would see it through.

Chapter

7

There are sockeye salmon who are hatched below the lake and who migrate to the sea shortly after losing their yolk sac. There are salmon hatched in the lake and who may be resident there for from one to four years. Sockeye born, as *Nerka* was, above the lake and who migrate to it in their first spring live through what is thought to be the more nearly normal sockeye pattern. But even for them there is no fixed period of lake residency. For some it is a single year, for others two, three and even four. *Nerka* was a two-year fish, which probably put him close to some kind of mean.

The spring thaw of his second year was late. The icegrip held into April, and even as May approached, the land was hard and the tree buds held tight. Bushes and trees that can be tricked too easily by an early but untruthful sun may die as the cold vise shuts again after a few days of deceitful warmth. On May 1 the thaw had barely gotten under way. The Coppertree's surface was still locked away from the sky. Deer tracks newly placed in the névé snow of wind-blow and recent refreeze sequences held their sharp edges for twenty-four hours and more. Then, one day, the temperature began to climb in earnest. As if they knew that this time it wasn't a trick, the buds, the billion buds of the Coppertree world peeked and then unfolded, and a soft yellow-green, the softest and most welcome color in nature unfolded against a faultlessly blue sky. Only the highest clouds passed that way for a full week and they were soft-edged scuds of cotton. A balmy wind rustled and brushed the land. For a few minutes one day, in the early afternoon, a gentle rain fell and it too was warm and cotton-textured like the air.

The ice on the lake had been thick and hard and the internal temperature remained low enough to hold the mass intact for several days after the true spring began. But even that last vestige had to give. In cannon-shot reverberations the ice cracked, jagged lines shot across and gentle winds rocked the resulting blocks. They ground each other and thudded against each other until new cracks appeared. Abandoned by its parent season, this once inexorable force was a toy to the sun. The brick-hard surface turned to mush, water bubbled up through the cracks and the lake began to spill over again in the annual rush down from above of winter waste and water trapped. In a week the ice was free and light poured into the surface waters and fingers of it probed deeper, even though there was turbulence and murk.

In his second summer *Nerka* would hold to deeper waters; there were many basins and several deeps. Each seemed to gather its own community of salmon fry and each could feed the host. With the spring breakup had come the inevitable explosion of plankton population. The fish ate ravenously and the mounting rings on their scales were becoming farther apart. It was the end of *Nerka*'s first winter band.

SOCKEYE

Each day of that second year *Nerka* ended the lives of other creatures and sped and flipped and turned to save his own. His whole day, in fact, consisted of that dual role, successful hunter and adroitly elusive prey. On one particular day, though, he nearly was killed by a new and unfamiliar predator.

There was a thudding against his side and it passed easily through his head until it drummed as well against his hidden ears. He saw nothing, it was too far away, and he could neither smell nor taste it. He drifted with a thousand other sockeye fry near the edge of a pasture of nearly microscopic crustaceans. He stopped eating abruptly as a confusion of signals reached him in a second wave. Then suddenly the incredible jaws, larger than any he had ever seen, exploded out in front of him through the mist of plankton before his nose. Long silvery threads stretched out in front of the monster and, strangely, light passed through it. Perhaps it was that, perhaps the fact that it threw no real shadow fooled the other fry into holding still until it was too late, until they were gobbled up and carried away. It rolled past *Nerka*, but only by inches. Like a score of others who fed beside him he was pushed away by a pulse of water that bunched up in front of the monster. He dived down as a funnel-shaped net towed on hundred-foot lines by a slowly trolling skiff gobbled up a large enough sample for the fisheries men to examine and by which they would estimate the year's lake population. Thousands of fry would die so that they could guess at how many millions there were. The sound of an outboard motor was thereafter engraved on *Nerka*'s secret memory. It was not a memory or a lesson he could ever be conscious of, but it was one he could respond to. He need never know it was there. Its presence plus his reflex pattern would assure him of life.

SOCKEYE

The second fall of *Nerka*'s life came after a period of furious growth. It was a brief harbinger, for just as winter had been slow to go that year it was quick to return. It had been chased away by spring, but held just beyond the trees, just across the northern tundra waiting for a crack in summer's northern wall. It was to be a bad year, a bad time across continents and oceans in the North. The snowy owls would push south in unusual numbers as the lemming population fell. Again, though, *Nerka* would sink to a deeper basin, a hole in the bottom of Coppertree Lake, and let the harshness pass. Less able to stand the shock of change than the creatures of land and air, he instinctively sank away from it. The vertical dimension of the fish's world spells survival.

As that second winter began to ebb (it would be a more gradual and dignified retreat than that of the preceding year), changes began to occur deep inside *Nerka*'s body. He began probing upward seeking for a signal while the activity of his pituitary-thyroid system increased. Some say it is the daily increase in sun hours that signals the change; others wonder if that is so. Something, though, tells the fish which are to migrate toward the sea that year to seek for a clue, to hunt until the system that integrates them with their cosmic world tells them it is time to go. What the small salmon was seeking was a breakthrough in the temperature barrier—an optimum of 41 degrees Fahrenheit. That would be the signal, that perhaps coupled with the lengthening day. As the water temperature rose toward that optimum, as the sun's rays pushed deeper for longer hours, the glandular activity accelerated and the thyroid-hormone level in his blood increased.

No one has ever figued out how the sockeye salmon can know that a saline sea lies below the furthest reaches of the river that flows from the lake in which they dwell as fry. It is almost too much to believe that fingers of salty scent and taste penetrate upstream to guide the fry. It is too much, but there is nothing else. If the fry can neither taste nor smell the ocean miles away, how do they know it is there? Yet they know it in a sure and foolproof way. The increased glandular activity predisposes them to seek the sea, to seek its salt and bitter taste. They are disposed to migrate and their tolerance for salinity increases. Before they even turn away from the lake, the changes occur within their basic chemistry. In the lake the fish need never *drink*, they need never ingest water. In the sea that will not be so, for the balance of salts in their own body will not so nearly match the one that surrounds them.

And then one day the signal came. Within hours salmon smolts by the millions began to move. From the vicinity of the single basin where *Nerka* had been holding, over two and a half million sockeye smolts began the move. They were going to the sea. They spilled out of the lake, they rose up from the basins and the deeper places, they passed millions of others whose time would come another year. They passed them and pushed for the gate, the lake's outlet stream. Predators played along the edges of their unguarded path, for the fish were too intent to be even normally aware. They were answering a call and a pull too profound; it blocked other things out. The edges of their mass were frayed by greedy larger fish, but *Nerka* was deep in the middle of the mass, deep in the heart of the throng of smolts. They were going to the sea, down from the lake, down from bear country and wolf land, down from the hills along a path as old as the species. The movement away from natal water was only less an imperative than that which would one day call the survivors home to die.

Chapter

8

The changes that *Nerka* would be called upon to make as he reached the sea were profound. They could not be accomplished in a few hours or even a few days and so they began in the lake before his departure, before the rush to the outlet stream and the descent to the Pacific world beyond the rolling stones and ocean shelf.

Under normal conditions the salt concentrates in a fish's body are greater than in the water around it. This was true of *Nerka* in the Coppertree system and that is why he did not need to imbibe water. There was a natural tendency for the water to flow into his tissues through osmosis, for that is the direction in which water naturally flows, toward the salt concentration. He lost chlorides, of course, through his kidneys and in his feces, but he had chloride-secreting cells to make up for the loss. The new chlorides were distributed throughout his body by his blood. In the sea it would be quite different. The salt concentration outside his body would be much higher and the flow of water would be away from his tissue. Unless he could compensate for that fact he could *dry out* in the middle of the sea.

SOCKEYE

In the sea he had to take water in, to drink and rid himself of excess salts through secreting cells hidden away in his gills. Water passing through was robbed of oxygen and enriched in chlorides. All of this had to be made ready, this chloride turnaround that made him a fish of two worlds. It was not a nicety or casual refinement, it was the difference, for *Nerka,* between living and dying.

The trip from the Coppertree basin deep, where he had wintered and awaited the spring freshet, to the sea was just over eighty miles. His trip would wind him through land no longer used by man, land of bear and fox and deer and the trails of Indians dead of malnutrition, measles, smallpox, syphilis and whiskey. The river itself changed character often. Where beaver had worked there would be broad ponds and strangely the main current of the river would push on across the center of them leaving small eddies to change places with water that had arrived hours before. It was spring and these places were at their deepest. They would be quieter come maximum sun.

At other places the land hunched its shoulders up around the stream, and a cut through harder rocks turned the stream into a race; broken boulders that had caved in from the walls over centuries of frost littered the bed. The smallest crack in the hardest rock can be expanded with the advent of water followed by freezing temperature. It is the microcreep of rock-ruin in a winter land.

In these fast places *Nerka* and the other smolt rode the race to the next quiet place. They could not swim, they could only point themselves with the current and swirl with it past rocks and submerged debris. The rocks were worn by centuries of pounding water and even when the small fish brushed them they would slide along and escape real injury. Fallen trees, though, were ragged and dangerous, and flotsam caught up in tangles meant for a world of air were traps. Smolt caught in them quickly drowned or were crushed. Luckily *Nerka* knew by instinct to keep to the faster middle water and to avoid the lure of a gentler eddy that could suck or whirl him into an accidental weir.

Raccoons and foxes moved along the banks as the millions of salmon smolt swept past. They pushed their muzzles into the mass of dead and dying fish caught in the tangles. A smolt alone was not worth the hunt but a mass of them pounded into a near-paste by thundering water and the bunching of more dead fish was a treat.

At last the thrust to the sea brought the smolt to a place where the land fell away in steps. One moment swirling forward in an accelerating stream and the next, in groups of hundreds, they were plummeting down seven and eight feet into pools. Pushed to the bottom by the weight of the water that carried them over the edge, they righted themselves and instantly reoriented themselves downstream. Pushing hard, they rose against the pounding above them and rode free on the far side of the pool, only to come again upon a rush that led to another fall and another pool. There were seven waterfalls over which *Nerka* had to plunge and whose slamming effects he had to survive. At last, after two days and nights of constant motion, he reached flatter land and broader, quieter waters. It was here he began to taste the first real wisps of chemical change. He had come to the place where the push of the ocean tide could flavor the river. The chemical adjustments in him began accelerating. He had very little time left before he had to become a fish of bitter water in a world as different from the Coppertree deeps as, perhaps, the sky is from the land.

SOCKEYE

A strange element in the life that *Nerka* had led so far was its absolute solitude. As an egg he had been hidden in gravel millimeters away from the others of his kind. As an alevin, too, his closeness to other sockeye was the thickness of a few sheets of paper. As a fry in the lake he had lived with millions of his kind and his paths had intersected those of millions more. In his descent through the maelstrom of the lower Coppertree in flood his adventures as a smolt had been shared with hundreds of thousands of young fish experiencing exactly what he was experiencing, undergoing the same tests. Their bodies brushed, they were hurled together, they fed together and very often, by the scores of thousands, they died together. In every way they were alike, yet each was as alone as if light years and not water molecules separated them. They actually shared nothing and never acknowledged each other. A fish does not know its identity and therefore cannot truly know the identity of another of its kind until it is time to breed; then smell overwhelms it and directs all of its actions and all of its energies.

It is true, of course, that different fish have different patterns, different ways in which they move and orient themselves to essential goals. Fish can align themselves so that schools of one kind can pass through and around schools of others. But it is wholly an unconscious thing, for a fish can never belong in a conscious way. A fish cannot learn from another fish any more than it can really learn very much from its own experiences. It may respond as a result of deeply traced response patterns, surely there are negative and positive incentives, but here again it is a question of reflex. A fish's reflexes learn what the fish itself can never know.

It was alone then that *Nerka* descended to the sea. Until

the act of mating occurred he would be a single dot of light in the Milky Way denying all other stars. He cared for his fellow fish as a star cares for a star and as the sparks relate to each other in a comet's ice-fire tail. *Nerka,* amid millions of his kind and thrust rudely into the world of billions of other creatures who could never taste sweet water and survive, would be alone. He read other sockeye as he read all that went on around him, but it was without knowledge of life, without the first inkling of concern or any power to know. All that he was had come to him at his hatching and all that he would ever be would wait until the hour when he again reached the redd where as an egg he had been fertilized and his chemical memory had begun. He had come to the sea with the single purpose of maturing—he would grow and mature and then, when ripeness again sent demanding messages throughout his glandular system, he would smell and taste his way home and use other cues as well. The spark was coming to the sea for it was his time to do so, his cosmic, eternal place in the cycle.

Chapter

9

The attrition along the route from Coppertree Lake to the last tidal reach of the Lower Coppertree River had been constant. There were fewer smolt now, fewer by many, many thousands. Most of the smolt didn't stop to feed once they started their migration downhill to the sea. They relaxed their usually alert defenses and were preyed upon all along the way. In fast streams fast cousins, trout, slashed through them and large gulping carpish fish swallowed among them with glassy-eyed indifference. Natural hazards chewed away at their numbers and only the best made it, the best and the luckiest.

The smell and the taste of the sea were the first clues *Nerka* received. Bitter threads of salinity worked back up into the river and it was along these ribbons of future and remembered taste that the young smolt moved toward their destiny. The sea taste became stronger by the hour; too, there was a two-way movement of water. It pushed inexorably toward the sea, but a second and equally inexorable force pushed back in an unremitting cycle of tidal activity. Water flowed across water in turbulent layers and the smolt had their first meeting with the moon.

SOCKEYE

For several hours *Nerka* held back while new sounds and sensations reached him in increasing crescendos. He circled and listened with his hidden ears and his lateral lines. He moved from place to place constantly reorienting himself. He was in a small tidal place, a small cut in the river's bank that formed a slow eddy and a quiet place to hold. His body was making the final adjustments and he was sufficiently keyed by the quality of the new water to automatically allow those adjustments time to occur. He was repacing his own body processes. Then it was dawn and *Nerka* moved out of the eddy and back into the main stream. The river broadened rapidly and surged with the sea beyond. Overhead gulls by the thousands gave rude noise to the sky, but *Nerka* was deep enough not to attract their attention. Smolt that somehow found themselves too close to the choppy river surface were often culled. It was quick and easy—suddenly a massive disturbance exploded through the surface and they were gone. Bubbles sank and then rose, but the young fish were already airborne in the gut of a bird no less rude now than before. Sometimes a gull would drop its prize and greedy warriors cut through the sky. The fish would become a toy, a thing to grab, to bounce and then to swallow.

The sounds were strange to *Nerka*, the pressures that played upon him in concert and fury. The thumping beat of a tanker off to the side, the thud-crush of a pile driver sinking the footings for a new pier at river edge. Beyond the mouth of the river, as *Nerka* approached, there was a gradient over which an incoming surf eternally rolled. Botton debris of shell and pebble and rock tumbled and surged, slushed and sighed and rattled. It was all new and in some strange way it excited *Nerka*. He pushed faster into the bitterness of the sea. Tasting his last truly sweet water for several years, he drove on directly ahead as the bottom fell away from him. He was in deeper water than he had ever experienced before.

As he pushed to sea he entered the Alaskan Coastal Domain. It would take him days to cross the area into the gyre to the south of it. He would then come to the vortex known as the Alaskan Gyral, and in that gentle elliptical vortex he would sample the truth of the sea and the promise of his inheritance. He was no longer a lake fish or a river fish. He had been transformed. He was an ocean fish, a marine animal, and all his chemistry was now completed. In those first hours he began to dehydrate as chlorides were sucked from his tissues, but he had been well prepared and before any appreciable harm was done he reversed the trend. He was drinking seawater and excreting salt beneath the opercula of his gills. His system completed the adjustments in time and this hazard, too, *Nerka* survived. Not all smolt do.

The waters of the Alaskan Coastal Domain drift westward along the south coast of the Alaskan Peninsula at a speed of eight to ten miles per day. They move along the top of the elliptical vortex that ends where the final Aleutian Islands stand in solitude among gull cry, sea mist and bleached grass. Here, too, are the shared memory of broken boats and broken men. Much of that water then swings north and east and circles the Bering Sea in a counterclockwise movement at a speed seldom exceeding two miles per day. It is a complicated system with some water from the Bering Sea moving almost due south at its western end in the East Kamchatka Current. Some of it moves eastward again along the southern edge of the Alaskan Gyral until it comes up against the coast of Canada and the United States. Through all of these currents and in all of

these worlds the salmon move during their years at sea. As
they sweep past coasts and islands they sense sweet water
from Asia and North America, from the Arctic and from
temperate zones, but only as fragments, only as highly
dilute hints. None of this attracts the fish to shore until they
are ripe with their time and then only that special sweet
water in which they grew. As thin as those dilute fragments of river systems may be, in the sea they are distin-
guishable to the salmon.

The top thirty feet of ocean held the most promise for
Nerka. It was summer and that upper zone was homoge-
nous, warmer and lower in salinity. The temperature
ranged between 50 and 54 degrees. A hundred feet down
the ocean was even more constant—it neither warmed nor
cooled and the salinity was almost 2 per cent greater.

Nerka shared his world now with a greater variety of
animals than ever before. His smallness was an advantage,
for many of the great animals that hunted in the coastal
waters off Alaska will only seek more satisfying prey. In
time he would interest them as well, but as a smolt new to
the sea he escaped their notice or at least did not sufficiently arouse them to trigger an attack. At one point the
sea around him seemed to explode. A wave struck him that
sent him spinning off in uncontrol. Over and over he
flopped although he fought to right himself. His whole
world—sight, touch, pressure, taste, scent—was full of
whale. *Orca*, a thirty-foot-long bull killer whale, cavorting
with a pod of his kind had flopped free of the ocean, gone
up into the air and then come down with tons of pressure.
It was this that had caught *Nerka*, flipped him and nearly
crushed him. Then up again, up came the killer whale
pushing a wake ahead that exploded with bubbles. Black
and white and uncounted thousands of times *Nerka*'s size,

the whale rose and again exploded past sending *Nerka* spinning away a second time. For several minutes the bubbles continued to rise as a silvery veil that lessened and slackened until the sea below returned to calm. The pod of whales were miles away by then doing something that *Nerka* could never do. They were playing, they were calling to each other, they were relating to each other and enjoying the sensation of life. They were interacting and even, perhaps, showing off. The salmon smolt and the killer whale were both sea animals but the one, the greater in size, was ahead in evolutionary gifts and skills. The history of *Nerka*'s kind had gone off on a different spur long, long before the killer whale's ancestral forms had even reached the land, much less returned to sea. But now it was back. As a mammal it was up from the reptile, in turn up from the oldest form, the fish. The killer whale, child of the fish, had some ancient ancestry in common with *Nerka*. It is a line that can be roughly drawn. But how different the form now, on encounter, how unequal the two perfections.

Chapter

10

No one has ever really traced the course of a sockeye
salmon at sea. That is a secret thing etched in deep and
secret places. It is likely that no two salmon ever live exactly the same life and that no two courses are ever repeated, although even the infinity of chance would seem
to be overwhelmed by the numbers of fish that come down
from all the freshwater systems that feed the northern Pacific world.

Nerka slipped westward early in his ocean career, then
south at the western end of the gyre and then east with the
vortex path. He was near the coast of the State of Washington, following a rising bottom and feeding well on a rich
harvest of tiny ocean life. The water was cold and cold
water sinks. Good vertical currents kept the layers that lay
upon each other from air to seabed richly fed with minerals. Life grows well in mineral-rich waters and life upon
life feeds in a slowly ascending scale.

At one point *Nerka* came upon a broken rocky place and
drifted among former mountains and over rents and frac-
tures of ten-thousand-year-old quakes and tremors. Some
of the spaces between the enormous boulders had filled

with sand. It was sand made there of disintegrating rock, for the tide and surf were strong, and sand carried to sea suspended in river water at flood. There were other shapes here, too, boats and ships tried too hard by weather. And on the decks and along the rusting plates of these artifacts of an inhabited coast the sand lay, too. Lines of rivets pushed up under the sand, some still barely showing, marching off into the murk like impossibly oriented mountains in miniature. It was a place of graves and abruptly ended history, a place for fish now, fish, their enemies and their prey.

There was a slushing sound, for the water was shallow enough and the surf above was felt below. The whole world rocked as it moved first in and then out, great surges of energy with a vast ocean behind them moving in against a sloping floor that led up, up to a continent beyond the furthest edge of the submerged shelf. From the distant gloom *Nerka* drifted into view. He turned one way and then another, a fish among many, of many kinds. He wasn't feeding at the moment, having recently found and taken the smolt of a different species, a small fish he was able to engulf. He rode the submarine swelling and let it lift him closer and closer to the battered hulk of a dead ship. Inside, the surfsurge rode through a narrow opening in the hull and played against a door that had been left ajar as the rammed and battered ship had overturned and died long ago. The door, rusty and growing thinner each hour of each year from the erosion of salt water, banged in a rhythm of the ocean push. It was a dull thud without echo, but it rang hollow and beat a tattoo that carried far and was heard by millions of creatures. And millions had come to investigate it. Predators had learned that, in time, without ever understanding it, of course; it was a place to prosper in. Sharks came here to feed and other creatures as well.

The thunk of rusty metal on rusty metal carried far away into the sea. It was an unfamiliar sound.

Nerka drifted closer and closer. As he passed across the side of the ship corpse barely inches above the plates, the swirling water hissed sand grain against sand grain and the shell and pebble debris that inevitably covers every horizontal surface in the sea. There was the slushing of the water itself, then its play on metal, the thud of the door within the hulk and the hiss of gravel. But then, suddenly, there was another sound. No man could have heard it, but a salmon could. It was as foreign to *Nerka* as the metallic rattle and groan of the dead ship. He could not locate it except that it seemed to rise up toward him. He held and turned first one way and then another, trying to obtain maximum purchase on the sound, using the tubes of his lateral lines and his hidden salmon ears. In fact, behind a tangled piece of hull not a dozen feet away a crab on extended legs moved sideways in search of food. He, though, was hunted even as he sought prey. An octopus, smartest and second-largest of the invertebrates (squid are bigger), pulled back and changed color until it was itself peeled paint and rusted metal. It pulled back, and the convulsions of its eight arms created a series of signals new to *Nerka* and one, indeed, that he might only rarely sense again.

Somehow the crab too awoke to danger and stalk-equipped eyes rotated in sweeping assessment of the immediate and always dangerous world. It froze in place, but it was too close and too late. The octopus, a monster fourteen feet across its outstretched arms, rotated its body until its beak pointed in the direction of the crab. The octopus shot out from its hiding place, snatched the crab and pulled it in toward a snapping, black parrot's beak. While alive the crab was pulled apart. The octopus did not need to envenomate its prey although it could have spit its deadly chemical down into the open wounds. Its beak stilled the crab forever.

The movements made by the crab and the octopus arrested *Nerka*'s forward movement. Repelled by the strange but clearly threatening movements and sounds, *Nerka* turned away quickly and vanished behind a section of up-folded iron plate. Sun played through rivet holes and lay dappling across the sand and shell beyond. *Nerka*'s sudden movement thwarted death again, for a very young shark on coastal patrol had dropped down from above and spotted the young salmon just before he moved. The shark fell upon an empty place and turned away in time to take another fish of *Nerka*'s kind who was just moving into view. It was an older fish and the shark bit it in half. The head was severed and sank to the seabed below where crabs who had not yet met their octopus would feed upon it. There was no one to observe the interesting fact that the face of a dead fish is no different, really, from the face of one that lives.

Nerka began his drift to the north again, beyond Washington State and the United States, along the fog-bound and high-treed coast of British Columbia. He drifted and grew, gained in size and strength and came each moment closer to the distant goal of maturity. A sea creature full and sure, he explored his world for hundreds of miles without curiosity or concern, drifting, marking the hours and the years with growth. His mission was to become complete and full of the nature of his kind so that he could make his deposit on the future and then die. His role, like the role of everything that lives, was immortality. He grew toward that, he escaped hazard almost every hour of every day, and that, too, was his gift to the future. In the sea his course was seemingly random; in time it was inexorably set and true.

Chapter

11

As *Nerka* grew, so did his power as a swimming animal. It is almost axiomatic that the larger a fish is the faster it can swim—and with each inch of growth *Nerka's* powers increased.

Muscle bundles lay along his body from head to tail whose full purpose was propulsion. He flexed sideways much more readily than he did up and down and was able to ripple the muscles along both sides in perfect coordination. A bundle contracting on one side would be matched by its exact counterpart expanding on the other. With body curve and rippling muscles along the length of his body, *Nerka* moved forward and ended each ripple with a thrust of his tail. That too drove him forward in the perfect symmetry of an animal in harmony with its medium. His streamlined shape allowed the water that naturally piled up in front of his head to slip free and flow along his sides as his muscles followed their rippling sequence. The flow added to his drive.

His tail, a fan-blade of thin bone rods covered by a stretched membrane, was attached to the end of his spine by a series of bony plates, muscles and controlling ligaments. It was as superbly a coordinated member as his senses and his lateral muscle bundles. It waved easily from side to side, and was always ready for an extra thrust toward life when death came close and offered itself for chance.

There is a kind of rule of thumb men use when they think of fish and wonder about them in the sea. A fish's sustainable speed is about seven miles an hour for every foot of body length. Men like such rules even though there are often more exceptions than creatures willing to submit to them. In the salmon, though, it is not far from true. There is another rule as well. A fish should be able to add 50 per cent again as much in a burst of speed. A one-foot fish, then, should "cruise" at from six to eight miles an hour and explode away from danger or come down on prey at from nine to twelve miles an hour. Salmon are faster than many fish; and *Nerka*, although still far from a foot in length, was yet nearing this power and this speed.

When *Nerka* moved quickly, for whatever purpose, he was called upon to make constant adjustments in his own chemistry. If he swam a normal easy course, moving without urgency from place to secret place, the metabolic wastes he built were removed by his bloodstream and passed away without special compensation. It was a chemical rhythm added to the mechanical, and together they constituted the system of his fish life.

But sudden bursts of energy, an explosive hunt or escape tactic, overrode such easy ways and a potentially deadly poison quickly began to accumulate in his tissues. After exertion *Nerka* would rest and allow the lactic acid to bleed away from his muscles and be carried off for disposal. As long as he lived, in the sea and in his eventual uphill fight to the far reaches of the Coppertree, he would balance exertion with rest and quiet his chemistry before exerting himself again. As a potentially highly active fish, he was more susceptible to this hazard than were many other species.

Nerka was equipped in another way for a highly active life. Like a number of fish he had a swim bladder which he could inflate or deplete to help control his buoyancy. Many fish, most perhaps, have swim bladders, tough little sacs deep inside of them, at their precise center of gravity. This provides them with the easiest means of trim; the least amount of work is thereby needed to remain level in the water. *Nerka* and his kind, though, have sacrificed that ease for a tactical advantage worthy of only the most active fish. *Nerka*'s swim bladder was below his center of gravity. When hovering he tended to be rolled up sideways, but he was muscular enough to compensate for that. When maneuvering in a current or when taking prey near the surface—or simply on a rising thrust—the off-center placement of this buoyancy compensator gave him great advantage. He could turn faster and harder than other fish, for on a bank the position of the sac tended to roll him on his side. Without extra effort he was in a position to use his forward motion to carry him around the curve, be it horizontal or vertically oriented, and on from there. If he broke to the surface, he could make an effortless 90-degree roll onto his side and in a single slashing movement go first up and then down. The arcs he could describe in the sea and would later use in countering river currents were things of swift beauty, the awesome purity of a life perfected by time. He was an athlete among fish, a lithe creature in the sea—for this he had been designed.

Nerka often traveled in company with others of his kind. They did not relate but sought the same conditions. They cruised to a depth of one hundred twenty feet although they swam more often in the last forty feet of ocean before the air began. The tended to concentrate in the subarctic zone of the northern Pacific, between forty and sixty degrees of North latitude. *Nerka*'s rate of travel varied; there were days when he moved no farther than fourteen miles in twenty-four hours and other times when he would travel as far as fifty. It would be several years before he would have anywhere to go except toward the next thing to stimulate or attract him, or away from the next set of stimuli to repel him. He was biding nature's time, preparing for his role.

The food *Nerka* sought, allowing for the differences between his two worlds, was not unlike that which he had hunted in the Coppertree system. Pelagic, planktonic copepods, amphipods and other minute invertebrates that drifted like clouds in nutrient-rich seas. He took young fish as well, herring at times, and other species. Larval crabs were a food often consumed and probably taken whenever encountered, and also the smallest of squid. As he grew he would take larger squid and larger fish, but always the crustaceans, the drifting clouds of animals, would be favored. He did not often rise wholly to the surface, but even when he fed just below it, his body roll would sometimes send his tail rippling half in air before he arced again into the ocean dark. There were times when he seemed to do things that had no real purpose and one is tempted to say he played, that he created pleasure and perhaps that complex affair we call fun. But we are not certain that this can be allowed a salmon.

He was becoming faster and more greedy. He fed constantly and he grew. He pursued food and smelled out waters where upwelling currents kept them rich and full of crustacea.

One day, if he survived to maturity, *Nerka* would be slightly over two feet long. A number of factors would influence not only the rate of his growth but his maximum size. The amount of food he consumed was paramount, but so was water temperature. It is believed that warmer waters foster greater growth, but many of the factors at work there are still secrets the salmon keep to themselves. There is a periodicity to the growth of *Nerka*'s kind, too, for salmon of one year seem to achieve greater size than salmon of another, even from the same river, perhaps from the same gravel beds and certainly as tenants of the self-same sea.

Maturity, too, a mystery of salmon life, when would it come? Heredity might be a factor, rate of growth another, or again a strange pulsing. On land the populations of animals vary markedly from year to year, and some see this as linked to cosmic happenings. If the salmon, too, are linked to events on distant bodies in the sky, they have kept that secret and we still search among those fragments of their lives we know for answers that only possibly are there. Some salmon mature not much after their second year and others when they are eight. It is at least strange, for they can be of the same species. And so *Nerka*, with all of these secrets inside him, swam north and then west again passing through galaxies of planktonic animals and consuming them as he moved, and through a world of shimmering bubbles, shards of sun diffused in a world of water, a world of life and a world of death. Trimming his buoyancy, moving vertically and horizontally through infinitely variable choices, bunching and relaxing muscle bundles, aiming himself, a silver dart, he swam the Pacific world, a secret animal in many a secret place.

Chapter

12

Nerka was to divide his ocean time between coastal zones and the incredible deeps farther from land, places where the ocean floor fell away from him in mile-deep increments. In each area he explored—and it was exploration without curiosity, nothing more, really, than the seeking of opportunity to match the season and the need—in each area there were new hazards. His kind is subject to infestation by at least forty-two different kinds of parasites for which the ocean has no cleansing effect. Heavily infested, a salmon can weaken, and a weakened fish is quickly served to a passing predator.

The larger *Nerka* grew and the more time he could spend away from the coastal areas, the greater his chances for survival. At times in his sweeping circuits of Pacific vortices he would cruise at depths of almost two hundred feet in water several thousand feet deeper than that. There, in the deep cool of the eternal sea-night, there was less danger and also fewer opportunities to feed. He followed planktonic layers, literally undulating blankets of food, as they rose and fell in the sea. Photophobic, these blankets would sink during the day but rise rapidly as the light above failed. In some seasons, with certain species predominating, the sheets of living organisms many feet thick would rise at a rate of a yard or two in as many minutes. *Nerka* and the other predators that survived on such small prey rose and fell with this tide.

Often in his travels *Nerka* would encounter the explosive effect of giant marine mammals, whales, porpoises, monsters cavorting and releasing crushing waves of energy that could be detected for miles. The relative quiet of the sea far from shore would suddenly fill with high-pitched trills and strange water-borne but somehow wholly disconnected wailings. The very sea would ululate, fill with the talk of giants chirping like birds over distances of miles. The sound would rise from below and sink from above, it would hammer in on all sides, and *Nerka,* following the pattern of other fish, would turn from side to side seeking direction and possibly avenues of escape. Below, on the bed of the sea, fish moved in close to the largest debris and when it was not too far away *Nerka* would sink down, too, and crowd in behind whatever masses were accumulated there. In mid-water, though, there was often no escape. Wail answered wail, whine came upon whine, and then the thumping would begin. Flexing their horizontal flukes up and down, pumping their enormous bodies forward at speeds far, far greater than most fish could achieve, the whales would pass by in noisy, social chorus. Never still, always calling to each other, linked and bound by a clear and all-encompassing social structure, they moved through the sea as not only the largest things that were but the most intelligent, the most advanced in every way. All other sea life folded back and opened the way to their thundering intrusion.

SOCKEYE

Often there would be killer whales. They were the noisiest of all, for they cavorted and played and their effect on the underwater world was a continuing peal of thunder and splash. Their great bodies rose and fell and twisted near the surface and then engaged in long sweeping arc-like dives. Pumping hard, they could swirl through a school of fish and with a single tail movement send tens of thousands spinning off into watery space. Some would be injured so badly they would soon fall prey to the first passing fish of large size. At times, when the fish were large enough, the killer whales would engulf them by the bucketful almost in sport.

It became roughest, though, when the killer whales were in pursuit of larger prey, other mammals, for then all was chaos and the water filled with blood and bits of flesh that attracted sharks and other larger fish. It was a time of extreme peril and all of the smaller fish sought escape. When, though, a dozen killer whales are in pursuit of a migrating group of seals, there is no escape. On one occasion *Nerka* sensed the movement of several score northern fur seals in an area of open sea. Females heavy with pups from the former year's breeding were moving north to the Pribilof Islands. They were nearly two weeks behind the movement of the bulls along the same avenues. The bulls had already reached the beaches and staked their territories. They pushed themselves up high on their front flippers and belched and bellowed impatiently. They were waiting for the females to arrive so that they could collect them into harems. The females would drop their pups almost immediately and then, within hours or days, breed again for the following year.

The females were moving fast for they, too, sensed the danger that was at hand. *Nerka* was sinking away from the seals, who were perhaps even more directly dangerous to him than the killer whales would be. But, before he had gone very many yards, the sea beneath him exploded. It was something he had experienced before, the thundering past of killer whales, but never so many, never this violent. They rose from below and swept through the small school of fish that sought to clear their way. They did not feed on the fish at all for their target was above, on the surface, frantically beating away in fruitless retreat. Other killer whales careened in on the surface and others leaped clear of the water and actually came down on top of the hapless cows.

The fur seal flock was decimated. They were bitten in half, torn apart. The younger killer whales, animals under ten feet in length, played with the scraps and rolled over and over with a head, or a flipper, or a tail section. In minutes over fifty seals died and fifty others that were not yet born. One hundred seals would not be missed on beaches where a million would gather (more than that would die on any one beach in the first week caught by the fury of fighting bulls), but in the sea it was mayhem. Seal blood, seal tissue spread throughout the water. The sharks came. In time they, too, began to boil the sea with their frenzy and the wave of death launched by the killer whale pod spread out. In minutes the seals were dead, in minutes more the killer whales were gone; but for hours the sea was discolored and more hazardous than ever, as marauders and scavengers moved through the site of slaughter. *Nerka* sank deeper than he usually did and held himself close near the disintegrating skull of another whale, a gray whale that had died there only two months before when another *Orca* pod had struck several of its kind. *Nerka* trimmed himself, adjusted his fins and held close to the massive jaws. Witness to death but not tragedy, slaughter but not cruelty, the end of lives but not wrong, *Nerka* held and waited and survived. In time he moved away from the skull, off across the bottom, and felt the familiar vibrations of other salmon as they moved past in a small school. He rose up toward them but turned away because they were larger than he was and he might do little more than feed one of them in a passing swipe of well-toothed jaws. He slipped down again to where the skull waited and held there yet a little longer.

Chapter

13

The giant submerged world through which *Nerka* moved
is of mysterious origin. It is, in fact, not yet understood
though the theories are endless. Ranging from inches deep
to incredible crushing depths of over seven miles, it is the
largest ocean system on this planet. In at least eight known
places its floor drops beyond the thirty-thousand-foot
mark. Its surface is believed to be in excess of seventy
million square miles, its islands are uncounted and its biomass, its population is beyond human reckoning.

Nerka was a part of this biomass of thousands of species.
He was of a highly mobile species; many other constituent
members of that mass lacked his ability to move up and
down and toward and away from continents. Across the
bottom in waters both deep and shallow the Asteroidea
crawled, sea stars of many and bizarre forms. They used
their arms to pull apart the shells of molluscs and extruded
their stomachs to engulf the fresh, living meat inside. Beneath the bottom, rubble worms burrowed and parted the
almost liquid sand. Often looking more like flowers than
animals, they pushed blindly on encompassing and assimi-

lating nutrient matter, flecks of organic material in the mud, the gravel and the sand. Sea cucumbers and other creatures that seemed only barely animal lay upon the sand, while shrimp of many kinds jetted above and massaged their water world with endlessly active appendages. In shallower places, and in some deep ones, anemones reached up with a thousand supplicating fingers, each studded with venomous darts making their flowerlike appearance all the more treacherous. Hydroids of many kinds formed on rocks and all other bottom debris. But in the world of *Nerka* there was no serious growth of coral, no reefs. Coral there was, to be sure, small animals and even small clusters of animals, but their distribution was markedly discontinuous. The Pacific Ocean has its coral reefs, giant formations like the Great Barrier Reef of Australia, but these monstrous assemblages occur only on the east coasts of major land masses, and that is true of all the reefs in the world. *Nerka*'s circuit was in the northern Pacific and off the west coast of a major land mass; these two factors precluded the possibility of his ever drifting into the strange and colorful world of the reef. That is a different kind of ocean and belongs to a different kind of fish. As mobile as he was, *Nerka* still functioned within marked limits.

Dangerous coelenterates, relatives of the corals and hydroids, floated in *Nerka*'s world, pulsing, pushing on in an endless circuit. Alternating between sexual and asexual generations, reproducing in astronomical numbers, they filled the sea with their filmy substance and died, as well, by the billions. Those that survived to become adults carried a deadly battery of weapons ever at the ready in food-seeking and defense. Their tentacles, often hanging down for yards below the Medusa bell, were equipped with capsules in each of which a coiled thread lay waiting bathed in a burning venom. There were thousands to each square centimeter. The slightest contact and each capsule would burst open and send its thread through the water to impale and intoxicate the nearest offender, or victim. *Nerka* avoided these flimsy masses. There would be days when none would be seen and others when the ocean seemed to be filled with stinging, primitive, invertebrate life. As far below the salmon as they may be in the evolutionary scale, the jellyfish can and will both kill and devour so swift and marvelous an animal as the sockeye. The jellyfish, mindless pulsing thing, knows the salmon in the sea-cycle way, as protein only and nothing more.

Of all the animals that drifted in the sea none were more important to *Nerka* than the diminutive crustaceans we call copepods, the "oar-footed" ones. The principal planktonic animal, they exist in scores of species and in astronomical numbers. Ranging in length from three to the inch down to seven-hundredths of an inch, they row their way through the sea with oarlike legs working in some strange kind of spastic sequence. They are the most important single link in the economy of the water in every kind of zone. Essentially oval in shape, with a small and undistinguished tail-like extension behind, they move forward with two antenna-like extensions protruding sideways from their unimpressive heads. In some species the oarlegs number eight and in others ten.

Their jerky movements attract predation and indeed that chore occupied much of *Nerka*'s time. Following their clouded thousands, millions and at times billions, he snapped at them like a terrier at a mouse and swallowed them one after the other in little gulps.

The copepod is an infinite resource in the sea because

its reproductive rate has been designed to accommodate the role of seabread to billions of other creatures. The mode of that reproduction in a strange way paralleled the experience *Nerka* would eventually have, for it was as impersonal and as imperative in its totally emotionless way.

The male and female copepod do not copulate. When it is time to breed, the male secretes a waxy-plastic substance from a special gland and shapes it into a bottle-like container. Into this container, which he clutches to him, he places his viable sperm. With this treasure ready he oars off in search of a female—and one is never very far away. Often the female will resist any effort on the part of the male to approach or touch her, but he eventually has his way, at times using force and special pincers modified to this vital task. The female has a small hole in the forwardmost section of her clearly segmented abdomen and it is over this hole that he attaches his treasure. Now sealed away from the sea by the mouth of the sperm bottle, it opens into a storage chamber, and upward into this the sperm now swim. Ducts lead from the chamber to the ovary. Eggs move down the ducts and are fertilized by the sperm before being extruded into the sea. In some copepods the fertilized eggs remain attached to the females; in others they float free to find their own route and destiny. Very often a female will absorb enough sperm from a single contact to last her throughout her spawning life. Others receive multiple spermatophores from a number of males.

The experience of the copepod may seem strange to mammals who know the moon and who care for each other in negative and positive ways, but if those strange ways should end the sea would die. The copepods on which *Nerka* fed for much of his life are at the bottom of the animal food scale and from them upward to man, each feeding upon each below, the chain is unbroken. The co-pepod, though minute, fragile and far from immortal, is an anchor to which all life is held by the pattern of the sea.

But the copepod, too, must eat. Below it in the order of sea and sea life are the diatoms, the microscopic plants whose population explodes periodically in numbers to rival the galaxies. Where the seas are most nutrient-rich the diatoms are most heavily concentrated. It is here the copepods seek their substance and here the other crea-tures follow in an endless chain we call the trophic scale. *Nerka* hunting and hunted was a link, one rather far up near the top. The larger he got, the more species he could hunt and the fewer that could hunt him, the farther up he moved. As a new animal in the sea, freshly down from the river, he was so small as to be hardly more than plankton himself. But as he fed upon the riches of the sea he emerged above that mass, and the older he got the fur-ther above it he climbed. With each day he became swifter, stronger, more capable and more dangerous to those other creatures in his sea who could never reach upward toward him. There was still hazard, though, for as he grew he became more visible to larger hunters, too, more worth their time to slash and kill. He passed through level after level taking larger prey and revealing himself to larger predators. Among them, of course, the shark.

Chapter

14

For all his time in the sea *Nerka* was the potential victim of a great sweeping presence. The sharks of his northern Pacific world were many and varied. The little-known sevengill shark was sometimes there, although usually alone and seldom seen. The sixgill, as much as twenty-six feet long, a killer of many fish, was often encountered and all that could would move away as quickly as possible. The thresher shark, twenty-five feet long at times and with a grotesquely elongated tail, was often encountered near the surface and would attack fish and other things it could find in the sea.

The salmon shark, too, was common. Seldom over ten feet long, it was nevertheless a full-bodied animal and a slayer of fish of salmon size. The basking shark was encountered and once *Nerka* came upon two dozen in an area of less than a square mile. Somehow *Nerka* knew and the other fish knew, too, that this giant was harmless. One of the largest of all the fish, the basking shark can reach forty-five feet in length: but it does not attack, it strains plankton by the ton from the sea with gill rakers.

The small brown cat shark, a fish about *Nerka's* size, usually kept to the bottom and was not often encountered. Something about its easy, inexorable movement disturbed *Nerka*, though, and he would move away when he sensed one nearby. Sharks have a particular way of moving and *Nerka* never failed to find it disturbing, never failed to gear himself for instant flight. No other fish parts water as a shark does, no other fish can so spread the sea wide in foray and patterns of kill.

In his sea, too, were blue shark, monsters elongated to twenty-five feet. Often traveling with or at least near many others of its kind, the blue shark is a voracious feeder. Giving birth to thirty or more living young at a time, they thickly populate the sea and slaughter millions of other fish every year, many of them salmon. The moment he sensed a circling blue shark, *Nerka* was gone, deep, far and fast. The presence of the blue shark was the presence of death, clearly marked and dreaded.

The soupfin shark swam in *Nerka's* sea, the Pacific dogfish and the terrible feeding monster, the Pacific sleeper shark. This last can approach twenty-five feet in length and will consume anything that falls in its way. It is never through eating and always ready to attack in great slashing motions.

All of these sharks are far more ancient fish than *Nerka's* kind. Barely changed at all in 350 million years, they move now as they did then, hunt now as then and kill as they have always killed. The largest of them have a brain the size of a walnut, and two-thirds of that, in true fish fashion, is given over to the single sense of smell. Even more alert than *Nerka* to chemical traces in the sea, the sharks can home in through turgid mists in an indistinct and clouded sea and arrive at the site of food barely sensed or seen.

Circling, always circling, they move beyond the range of most other creatures' senses, tasting their targets long before they ingest them. It is the eternal sampling that keeps the shark so well fed and sustains the quality of unending cold-eyed menace.

Once a shark starts to circle, anything on which it plans to feed is in trouble. The shark is usually the more acute, primitive though it may be. Capable of frenzy once the feeding has begun, a group of sharks—whether school or loose feeding association no one seems to know for sure—can tear a true school of fish apart and cut them in two by the hundreds in slashing, driving invasions of hunger and ancient skills.

The shark is so old a form that it does not even have real bones. It is a cartilaginous fish with denticles and taste buds imbedded in its seemingly scaleless skin.

No shark was more adept at attacking other fish than the bizarre thresher shark. *Alopias* has a tail, at least the upper half of a tail, as long as his body. Blunt-headed, he is often seen over fifteen feet long, at times much larger than that, and he feeds near the surface. Other sharks feeding deeper often drive schooling fish upward and the thresher is said to circle them and move his incredible tail, at times ten feet long, back and forth herding, as it were, the fish inward in panic. They feel his tail before they see him and then suddenly from somewhere on the perimeter of the circle being drawn in the sea there is an eruption and blunt-headed, hard, empty-eyed *Alopias* is upon his massed prey. It is an easily done thing, this descent upon fish herded together in panic, and it is soon over. The great and ancient *Alopias* moves away, and the school in fragments hangs in the water victimized by other sharks that have felt the troubled action from great distances and have moved in to share the feast. The fish are stunned, too often so stunned they fail to move away.

In all his years in the sea, *Nerka* was seldom far from a shark of one kind or another. He sensed them as he was equipped to do and he feared them in the same way, for in a salmon with rich meat in thick bundles along his sides the fear of the shark, the automatic response to that presence in the ocean, is equipment as surely as a gill cover, a fin and an eye to see.

Nor far off the coast of British Columbia, on yet another of his circuits, *Nerka* drifted lazily through a galactic mass of crustaceans feeding at ease and sensing no great danger at hand. Then, slowly at first, there came up to him from below the sense of massive movement. A school of pilchard had gone deep in the presence of some earlier surface threat and were now coasting across the bottom of a flat-bedded area. Something, though, was troubling them and with vibrations and perhaps in ways we cannot guess they broadcast their concern into the ocean around them. The closer together the pilchard pushed, the more troubled their signals became, and then the explosion hit. Seven blue shark came down upon the massed fish and struck before they could effectively scatter. Pilchard, or Pacific sardine, shot off through the surrounding water like fragments of a grenade and the signals struck *Nerka* hard. A thousand other fish in middle waters there also got the message of catastrophe and scattered. *Nerka* fled among them. But other sharks were near, too, and they began to home in on the flashing stragglers. It was one of the closest brushes with death *Nerka* had ever known, for as he beat away with the rest a salmon shark well snouted and intent on a meal descended mouth agape. He struck at *Nerka* as he passed, but there were other fish there as well and although *Nerka* received a slashing wound it was another salmon, one only slightly larger than *Nerka,* that died instead. *Nerka* began to sink at once, for muscles were cut and he found it difficult to flex properly and hold his trim. With his forward motion impaired he sank away from the scene of carnage, sank deep to where some bottom weeds offered a degree of protection. A shark's snout could have easily parted his simple retreat and had him but there was too much going on above and *Nerka* managed to sink away without attracting attention. He was losing some blood and this could have attracted the acutely sensitive sharks had not the sea been soaked in blood and froth from the savage meal of pilchard and other fish unlucky enough to be nearby when the great storm of sharks burst upon them.

Nerka hung there, working mostly to keep trim and not float up onto his side. He maintained his trim, he hid as far into the weeds as he could, and he held. His every instinct was to live. In his own primitive way he knew he was sick and would yet become sicker before he began to get well, if indeed that was to be the outcome. *Nerka* held, held as he hid and waited to see if he would die there. As for the mother sea itself, it did not matter at all. One way or the other those chemicals in use by *Nerka* as a living thing would come back. There and then, or down the river above the Coppertree, the ocean could wait.

Chapter

15

Near where *Nerka* held and waited for a decision from fate, other fish were carrying forward their species each according to its own style. Immediately off to *Nerka*'s side grotesque midshipman males guarded their eggs with seemingly absurd intensity. It was spring and the females had glued their yellow, globular eggs to the undersides of rocks and shells and other bottom matter. The twelve- to fifteen-inch males, with bulging eyes and prominently toothed bottom jaws, shot out and threatened *Nerka*, so he moved away. He was set upon by others of their kind and he moved away again. Given a territory and as firm a foothold on eternity as a fertilized egg, even the smallest fish becomes an aggressive monster.

The flow of blood had stopped and the knitting had begun. Within hours *Nerka* was building cells from within and sealing off vital tissues from the sea. He was stiff, and flexing in full movement was still not possible. He used as little energy as he could and followed an ascending slope again, up toward a continent although that was still many miles away.

SOCKEYE

Sole undulated across the bottom wherever *Nerka* moved, ovate sole and others more elogate. Gremlin-like, twisted with eyes askew, changing color and often pattern they scurried from place to place cryptic, darting and frightened. Rude sea perch of many kinds, turning from side to side, rushed in to *Nerka* and as quickly rushed away. They were a bother but their aggression was nothing more than show. In the sea animals display to each other and signal each other perhaps no less than on land or in the sky. Of course, to truly read a fish one should own the fish's eyes, the fish's ears and the creature's compulsions and imperatives as well. Fish speak to fish and not to man.

Nerka continued to heal but still he held to cover. Even the slashing appearance of bonito nearby did not frighten him into revealing himself in flight. The great disturbance caused by these highly active three-foot fish passed over and around him and he sensed it all, but still he moved slowly up the slope as they went off to worry another part of the sea. He began to taste the thin sweet water from the land. On the slope, far from the lowest tidemark, some sweet water seeped up into the sea. *Nerka* passed through these streams and minijets and a memory was piqued, for just a few moments, a memory was there, but he was not ready for it and there was yet neither taunt nor tug.

At one point an alarm came through the sea and *Nerka* moved as quickly as he could toward an upended slab of stone. He pushed in hard near its bottom and held as a swarm of barracuda swept by in middle water. It was June, though, and they were headed to the open sea to spawn. They had been sweeping along the shelf feeding on the rich life there but now there were new demands and none would stop to feed. Still, *Nerka* held fast until they were gone. He was aware of their movement pattern and like the shark they spelled threat. Fast and greedy, powerful and forever hungry, they of the long jaws meant death for any fish in their way. *Nerka* had become a good barracuda-sized meal. His growth had brought him to that.

Twice in his slow ascent up the shelf away from the sea *Nerka* encountered the strange and disturbing sensation of writhing that the octopus imparts. In both cases *Nerka* turned away. At times young sardines, anchovies and jack mackerel passed over him in clouds. There were millions of the infant fish flashing silvery lights in all directions, but *Nerka* had not yet resumed the pursuit of active prey. He was feeding, though, gulping crustacea that hung in the water near him and even on a few occasions worms that he plucked from the sand. It is the history-imparted genius of wild things to conserve energy when they are ill and it was this that *Nerka* practiced. Even with his shallow eyes and feeble brain he could sense beyond a meal to eternity.

The healing was going well; hour by hour, day by day, his strength returned. The more of this he felt the more he fed, the more prey he took. One element of improvement fed the other, and he began again to seek a wider diversity of prey: arrow worms and copepods, amphipods and the eggs of many fish. Bivalve larvae, snails and other inver-tebrates. Then he began on fish again, anchovy and sardine young at first, then the more active jack mackerel young and even a few salmon smolt. Along the shelf there was great variety to choose from.

There would always be a white scar where the teeth of the shark had grazed *Nerka*'s side but the muscle bundles below had healed. He could once again flex his body from side to side and snap his tail in a gesture of speed. He eased his ascent toward the land and then, one morning, he turned back toward the sea. Feeding as he went, he slipped down the shelf and chose middle water a hundred feet off the floor at first and then a hundred fathoms, and soon the bottom was too far away to matter. There were still sharks nearby and *Orca* not many miles away, but *Nerka*, repaired and ready again, pushed off into the sea and turned north to linger the summer on the underside of Alaska. From there he would push to the West and by the time snow was falling on the Coppertree system he would be off the Asian coast. His travels were profound and the distance covered was in the thousands of miles. For such feats he needed his strength, he needed the drive of those muscles that could flex his body and send him arcing after prey.

Chapter

16

There are giant animals in the sea and giant plants, too. What the whales are to the copepods, the world's largest brown algae are to the diatoms on which the copepod feed. Known as kelp or simply seaweed, these massive plants often exceed one hundred feet in length. Great masses of such primitive plants form submerged forests and *Nerka* often drifted along their seaward edge. Only on the brightest sunlit days could even the thinnest rays penetrate for more than a few feet into the glistening jungle of submerged growth. Leaflike blades connected to a central stalk waved slowly in the sea gracefully etching each current, each nuance of water-thrust and shove. The stalks were firmly glued to rocks at the bottom of the sea and in that tangle a whole vast community of animals lived, many only for the hours of their own infancy, for there it was safe and few animals dared challenge the mass. Rounded air bladders—nothing more, really, than expanded and hollow sections of the stalk—held the heads of the floating algae giants aloft and pushed them toward the meager sun. Small bags of gas, they yet defied the sea.

SOCKEYE

The great kelp plants extracted chemical elements from the sea—potassium and iodine among them—and their tissues were rich in a variety of compounds valuable to man. In other parts of the world they are harvested by the thousands of tons but not these beds, not where *Nerka* roamed. Reproducing sexually, free-swimming sperm surrounding and finally penetrating eggs either still within cavities in the plant or motile in the sea, these plants produce uncounted numbers of zygotes each year that attach themselves to rocks and then grow directly into new plants. Occasionally whales, occasionally ships and often heavy seas destroy vast areas of kelp growth; like a forest fire, sea forces can rip through a submerged world and create havoc among all that lives. But the brown algae called kelp is an eternally self-renewing resource, and the great swaying, undulating forests of slick brown are always there stretching their lazy, greasy figures in the sea.

There were other plants, too, in the world through which *Nerka* moved—fungi, phytoplankton and even seed plants like eelgrass. But the algae predominated—over five hundred species off the coast of British Columbia alone. The plants that died fed the thick broth of the sea and were fed upon by a myriad of creatures that variously bored and sucked and absorbed chemical-rich plant substance and then fed the higher animals on the scale. *Fucus, Codium, Porphyra, Ulva, Nereocystis, Gracilariopsis,* far more than sweet sounds of ancient Latin and Greek—galaxies of plant life that lived on the sea and fed the sea and discharged sperm and egg and intermediate forms into the water by the ton. Feeding, pulling chemicals from the water and introducing others, fed upon and used and entering and reentering the cycle in infinite repetition, they gathered up behind *Nerka* and helped him push forward in growth and in the accumulation of strength and power. One day, in the stream above the Coppertree, in the farthest reaches of that sweet water system, their substance would be planted in egg and seed and sea futures. That substance would not appear as baby plants to replicate the parent form but as salmon, alevin, fry, parr and smolt.

As *Nerka* cruised along the edge of great forest stands, he encountered one of the most frolicsome of all the creatures in the sea. If there is a sense of humor anywhere in the ocean it belongs to "the priceless one," he whose pelt caused Alaska to be explored and colonized and in the pursuit of whom a thousand men died. Amid the kelp were the sea otters, the giant marine weasels whose pelt was once reserved, on pain of death, for kings and emperors and women of particular softness.

No more valuable fur has ever been known than that of these giant marine weasels. Russian and Chinese emperors and lords of war demanded their skins at whatever cost in human life, and indeed the salmon rivers of the American Northwest were rediscovered by men who came there in pursuit of this incredible animal. Unlike other members of the weasel tribe, the sea otter does not have a subcutaneous layer of fat to protect it from freezing water. That work is wholly done by fur so fine that when it is wet you can run your fingers through it with your eyes closed and never be certain when you are touching it and when you are not.

The sea otter is everything a salmon is not. It is required by life-style and evolutionary place to be acute, aware, alert and ready. These qualities automatically raise intelligence to such a level that fun is possible and play quite probably a necessity. The sea otter may be somber one minute but is lively and frolicsome the next. The salmon lives because it must, because that is the direction in which it was aimed at birth—toward death through life—but the sea otter *enjoys* life and plays games with strands of kelp and with others and with the sea.

Nerka, skirting a forest of kelp one brilliantly sunlit day, came upon a pocket population of otter some thirty in number. It was the kind of day when the sun touched the sea with a spilling of golden light. The surface of the water was pocked in a million places by the tops of kelp strands that bent over and lay parallel with the surface just barely and not always submerged. In among those indistinct and always moving intrusions the otters floated, mostly on their backs and mostly simply dozing in the sun. Babies lay splayed on their mothers' chests and bellies and occasionally rolled off for a minute or two in the sea before climbing back aboard. Periodically the otters, one or two at a time, would roll over and disappear. Dropping down through the tangle of kelp where few other animals their size could negotiate a safe passage, they reached the bottom streaming bubbles behind and there searched for urchins and shellfish. Some rose to the surface with both a meal and a stone tightly grasped by their front legs. Their webbed hind feet easily drove them upward still streaming silver bubbles from their fur. On the surface they would roll over, maneuver the stone into place on their chests, and proceed to pound the shellfish on the improvised anvil using both front feet to grasp it. Eventually the shell would give and the tender meat inside would surrender up to the otters, ravenous animals that have to eat a quarter their weight each day in order to survive.

At times one otter would set out in pursuit of another and there would be a chase through the slippery kelp and deep into the equally slippery sea. It was play, and although there was danger to the slower moving fish it was harmless and worked to tie the otters together in relationships unknown to salmon but essential to a weasel that has gone to sea. Otters cavorting, diving and rolling will take a fish, but usually of the more lumbering kind. Salmon, when careless, can be taken too and their sweet flesh is welcome; but *Nerka* was repaired and well and swift and one playful pass by a diving otter was easy to avoid. The next time *Nerka* encountered the animal it was surfacing, rushing past with a rock under one foreleg and a sea urchin under the other. It shot past and left *Nerka* to swim through a rising stream of bubbles, the passing mark of the sea otter upon its liquid world.

Pushing west from there, heading out again to where the vortex awaited to carry him once more through a slow turning, *Nerka* encountered one of the strangest fish in all the oceans of the world. Rare there but sometimes seen, a giant *Mola* cruised just below the surface. The ocean sunfish, *Mola mola* in fact, with its short body, deep and ovate, enormously compressed and seemingly with no tail, floated as if unaware of anything else in the world. Small-eyed, over nine feet long, it moved first right and then left, but only slightly, and seemed to seek a current that would free it of all effort. The high dorsal and anal fins were like blades that marked the disclike creature and made it seem a fish at all. Small-brained even for a fish, it seemed detached and unbelonging. It was a female and the giant ovaries contained an unthinkable 300 million eggs. Soon they would be ripe and would join the water, there to hatch into larva no more than one-tenth of an inch long. Those very few of that incredible number that survived would no more resemble their mother at first than the mother did the other fish of the sea.

The great *Mola* cast a shadow, was a gray presence, and

SOCKEYE

Nerka moved over close to where the form hove into view. Moving along beside it *Nerka* fed on the host of smaller creatures that inevitably gather near any larger body in the water. But then *Nerka* felt the signals. A thousand times faster and more certain than the *Mola*, *Nerka* swept away. He dropped and turned and fled before the signals that came careening toward him through the molecules of the ocean, through the particles of the sea. *Nerka* was half a mile away when the *Orca* pod struck. The *Mola*, a ton in weight, was thrown clear of the water and fell back into total and instant destruction. She died there and fed the killer whales. Her 300 million infant young not yet made whole died with her. But one of the killer whales carried a young inside of her and he would soon be born. Nature reckoned it a fair trade, 300 million of one kind for one of another. It was the kind of trade that makes a sea system work. And that kind of system is the one that would one day feed *Nerka* back to a continent in trade, too—for smolt of another year. The sea is an auction block every hour of every day. There is only one ultimate bidder and that is the sea itself . . .

With the *Mola* gone, and the *Orca* away calling and hunting the kelp beds for otter far coastward to the rear, *Nerka* swung west again. The Pacific was before him, the sea and yet another year in which to grow.

Chapter

17

The concept of man, much less the danger he posed, was far beyond the reach of *Nerka*'s relationship with his Pacific world. To conceive of man *Nerka* would first have had to perceive of himself and then make the comparison, for just as man sees the fish in contrast to himself—in the ways it differs from him—so, too, the salmon would need the corresponding baseline. *Nerka* did not and could never have any so advanced an intellectual tool. There was no *I* in his world, no *me* and therefore no *he* or *him*.

Man for *Nerka* was a series of totally unrelated stimuli and as a salmon he reacted in salmon ways to each as each arose, flourished and vanished. In no way did he connect them to an overall phenomenon, in no way did the land creature that became a sometime sea thing intrude as a total reality. One day man was a sour taste in the sea where bunker oil was slushed overboard to combine with sea and salt and sun to become a hideous giant and very black amoeba creeping beachward along a fouling track. On another day man was a thudding thump, a pounding of one screw, two or even three as a ship pushed through a rolling sea and aimed itself to a distant place of commercial moment. Smaller boats, too, existed as distinctive if lesser thud-thunks that could drift down on a salmon from above and be variously alarming or curious or, in time, familiar and ignorable. Man was also the dead ship in the sea, or a stream of bubbles and a lumbering apparition wheezing and hissing out of the gloom, as on the one occasion *Nerka* happened upon a salvage diver. One day early in his marine career, *Nerka* happened upon man in another form. A great net was drawn through the sea and then began closing like a drawstring bag. Thousands of fish were trapped and crushed together as the world collapsed inward on them and began tugging away toward the surface and the suffocation of dry air. *Nerka* had been near the mouth of the closing trap, near it but not in it, and he was caught up in the headlong flight of a thousand escaping fish and even porpoises that burst away and created a hammering tide in the sea that nothing could resist. *Nerka* was swept along and away and escaped, although it took him over an hour to adjust his internal chemistry from the shock of the encounter. Still there was no reality to it that could be called man. Salmon have no names for the pressures and the scares of their world.

At times man was garbage dumped at sea and the sharks that followed that stream of swill that bobbed at and near the surface. Man was a blue plastic bottle and a red plastic place mat, a steel can and an aluminum pail. He was, too, a glass net float and a large plastic geegaw of many colors designed to appear like a sea creature that never was and never could be. In a thousand ways variously blatant and subtle man marked the sea world of *Nerka*.

Once far at sea *Nerka* floated ten fathoms down and picked casually among several undulating layers of plankton. Creatures of increasing size on an eternal gradient of living tissue fed on those just below and *Nerka* was in there, too, large and greedy but so stuffed that he snapped up only what was handiest and that more by reflex than need or intent. He swam between two layers of crustacea and moved up toward one, fed along the bottom of the cloud and then drifted down to nibble along the top of the other. It was late in the afternoon and the ribbons of photophobic creatures began their ascent through the cool and the dark of the blue-green world. The red end of the spectrum died completely above, killed by absorption long before it reached down to where *Nerka* fed.

Ahead of him, well beyond his sight, there were plopping signals at the surface, small destructions of peace at the air boundary followed by hissing sounds as lead weights tugged forward and drew mile-long strings into the sea. Above, a line of boats drew a network on the surface moving slowly and with little noise. *Nerka* was too deep to pay much attention, for the ships in the failing light cast little in the way of shadow and the sounds themselves had often registered before without causing pain and so could be ignored.

Slowing, *Nerka* moved along the carpets of copepods toward the trailing and almost invisible strings in the sea. He sensed an unusual presence in only the most casual way, and it failed to alarm him. It meant nothing, was part of nothing that had gone before, and so *Nerka* floated toward them, and the distance closed.

Now a signal did reach him. There was raw flesh, anchovies and other species, fresh raw food like the kind he sensed when sharks and killer whales fed and left the sea soaked with the inside juices of edible creatures. Hunks of flesh hung in the sea and their juices welled out and drifted away. They hung from the almost invisible and in no way threatening threads and drew *Nerka* in. Others, other threads and other suspended hunks of flesh drew other fish in for miles around. The sea was well baited and the fishing fleet settled above to wait. Their game was waiting once the long lines were over the side, baited, set and receptive.

Nerka struck a baited hook thirty feet below the surface. He had been rising when he finally encountered the first line. He rose up through the gloom toward a piece of flesh that dangled free looking silvery and slightly phosphorescent in the darkening water. It excited him and he rose up under it and snapped it up. He turned his head by arching sideways from midway along the length of his body and was about to swallow his latest meal when he tasted the treble hook over which the flesh of the sacrificed fish had been drawn. He had swallowed water when he first took the bait into his mouth and was in the process of sluicing it out from under his gills. His effort to eject the bait with its hook was a single beat off. He had already turned far enough and the hook had set in the corner of his mouth. Behind a bony plate, behind a string of tough cartilage, the hook broke through the wall and refused to back out. *Nerka* pulled back but he couldn't let go of his attempted meal. He rose up but still it was lodged, his meal would not let go of him. When pulling back and rising up would not work, *Nerka* dropped down rapidly and although there was some little play in the line that rose above and dropped below him into invisible depths he was soon pulled up short again. For a moment he allowed his trim to vanish and floated on his side, belly trying to rise above his back. He trimmed, though, he contracted muscles and moved a stream of gas and righted himself and tried to back away again. The hole in his upper jaw was enlarging, ripping under the effort he was making, but he was far from free.

Nerka fought for several minutes trying to eject the now-pulverized meat from his mouth. He turned and twisted as far as he could go, pulled back and tried to charge past, but in time he began to tire. Again, acids were building up in his muscle tissue and the effects were beginning to tell.

The sun had gone from the sky above and the sea was dark. Only the lighted creatures cast beacons now, the bioluminescent organisms that winked and blinked their own brief galaxies into being. Several times *Nerka* came to life and began his battles over again. As he agitated the water around him it lit up with tiny creatures who glowed at the slightest disturbance. Bathed in the eerie cold light of the nighttime sea, *Nerka* fought on.

Hundreds of fish had been trapped in much the same way *Nerka* had been. For miles around they, too, thrashed and tugged and died silently. Their thrashings reached *Nerka* and his reached them. In total they sent an unmistakable signal out through the sea, animals in trouble, and onto those signals the sharks were quick to lock their hunger and their intent. The sharks fed along the lines, ripping first one fish free and then the one above and up. The bigger the fish the more violent the tugs and battles to tear the dead and dying away.

Larger sharks came too, and brushed past the smaller and even some of the smaller sharks were taken. Sharks drifting back and forth and up and down brushed the lines, tangled in some as they became more frantically involved in their feeding, and as the feeding approached the frenzied level the lines shook from top to bottom. The men in the boats cursed and started the winches. They knew how many hooks they would find with nothing but the heads attached, for there was the kind of carnage below that makes fishermen hate sharks.

A blue shark over thirteen feet long was feeding up the

line to which *Nerka*'s deadly bait had been attached. He had a gut full of headless fish when several smaller sharks, blues as well, drifted in and began to feed along the same line. The larger blue, almost three hundred fifty pounds in weight, struck out at them and in so doing tangled the line around his tail. He twisted and quickly pulled free, but an enormous convulsive wave ran the length of the line all the way to the surface. *Nerka*, who had been aware of the shark feeding up from below for several minutes, was pulling back to the full limit of his strength when the wave came looping along the line, snaking its energy toward the surface of the sea. His position was exactly right and the hook tore free. The small piece of fish flesh that had drawn *Nerka* into and onto the hook floated away and so did a piece of his own jaw. It was, all said, a small injury, but *Nerka* was sickened by his exertions and he rolled over and dropped away into the sea. He sank, found it difficult to right himself, but finally managed to do so. Above and behind him the large shark continued his devastation all along the line, and the boat's winches began dragging up the signs of the struggles and the savage destruction that had taken place. *Nerka* continued to drift away; in a very deep place he came to rest behind a mass of bottom rubble. He held there and waited. He would have to wait to see if he was to live or die. The process was beyond him. If he were a strong enough salmon his system would work sufficiently well toward the chemical equilibrium that meant life. If he was strong enough he would live and then leave the sea. His time had come. His terrible struggles on the line in the sea had come on the eve of his maturity. In the world above spring was approaching and it was the spring of *Nerka*'s return from the sea. But first he had to wait.

Chapter

18

Nerka lived. His jaw was disfigured but not so badly that he could not feed. He was sick, but he lived on and remained deep and avoided all contact with other fish he sensed near him and above, between his position of retreat and the sky. He did not know what had hurt him and if he again encountered a long line floating on the surface dangling its thousand anchovy-baited hooks or anchored deep with fierce treble hooks at the ready, he would be likely to succumb again. The line itself was too indistinct, too vague for him to learn from it. He would be safe from the long line only if he did not encounter another of its kind.

It was once believed that the species of Pacific salmon traveled only very short distances in the sea, that their journey was to the continental shelf and no farther. It was easier to believe that, for then there was a smaller and more compact mystery in their return home. A fish halfway between Asia and North America is mysterious indeed, for the streams it has available to it number in the tens of thousands and the trip from mid-ocean to natal redd is a maze whose complexities defy description.

SOCKEYE

That was the task that now faced *Nerka*. He was far into the Pacific, well beyond the continental shelf, and if his life was to have any meaning he would have to face this final seemingly insurmountable task. While still avoiding the hazards he had known all his life, while still hunting effectively enough to maintain condition for the terrible strains that faced him at the end of his journey, he would have to find his way.

There were endless configurations of chance in *Nerka*'s world, but those things that happened inside his own body were exquisitely timed. There was no chance there at all. He would cover as much as thirty miles a day on his homeward migration. Since he would not migrate seriously for much over eight hours out of each twenty-four, it is believed, he would have to maintain speeds of between three and four miles an hour—this despite any currents he might encounter. He was now racing a cosmic clock and a universal cycle.

Inside his body his testes were ripening. The tubules inside each were thickening and filling out the interstitial space that had always existed between them. Soon the tubules would be full enough, thick enough to discharge large individual cells, and these in turn would begin a series of divisions that would culminate in active sperm. By the time this process was completed he would have to be at that one place in this entire Cosmos where their potential could be used. Throughout his body, glands were discharging the chemical signals that told him what he must do no matter what the obstacles, what the risk. In fact there was no risk at all. The moment the first signals were given, *Nerka* was doomed. Beyond the ripening testes, beyond the thickening tubules and the cell divisions, beyond the sperm and the rituals and the exertions there was only death. This was the final phase of *Nerka*'s life and no power on earth could extend that life or change that course. His life was mounting to a crescendo before collapsing completely in the stream where he was born. He was facing both the climax and the sole purpose of salmon life.

Many changes would take place in *Nerka* as he fought his way back through the sea, back up his river and onto the gravel bed where he first appeared as a living form. His jaws would elongate, bit by bit they would grow longer and more fierce-looking. His snout, once a smooth and easy shape, would become hooked and add to his ferocious appearance. By the time he reached his native stream, he would have far longer teeth than those he had had even as he approached maximum size in the depths of the sea. His body would become more compressed laterally and he would develop a pronounced hump on his back under his dorsal fin. Strangely his skin would thicken, as the days of his journey passed, and perhaps even more strangely his scales would be largely absorbed into his body. And there would be striking color changes too. Once silvery slate, he would arrive on his spawning grounds bright red in color with olive-green markings on his head and tail.

The reasons for all these changes are not fully understood. They have been speculated upon since observations by Darwin and indeed there are many secrets here. Perhaps the elongated jaws, the hooked snout and the enlarged teeth are for fighting between the males, perhaps the vivid color changes and the pronounced hump are to attract females and repel enemies. Perhaps, but we cannot be sure.

The color changes may have other values, for the sockeye returning from the sea is re-ascending into water with reduced oxygen content. There would be reduced gill respiration, less oxygen taken in that way. As the efficiency of the gills became less, *Nerka* would require an increase of oxygen from other sources so that he could survive the final exertions and fulfill his goal. In the sea he opened his mouth forty times every minute. Each time his mouth closed, completing a cycle in effect, his opercula or gill covers would open. Inside, red gill rakers would admit oxygen from the water. In his stream this would not be enough.

The color changes could mean an increase in carotenoid and lipoid pigments in his muscle and skin tissues. These pigments are efficient carriers of oxygen and efficient catalysts as well in the complex process of oxidation reduction. All of this would make the uptake of oxygen from the external environment much more efficient than was needed at any other phase in *Nerka*'s life. These, then, could be merely morphological and biochemical prerequisites for *Nerka* to function in those final hours. All the rest could be our projection from the fierce, hot look of the salmon ascending to breed.

But the color changes, the glandular exchanges and cross-signaling, the strange morphological changes were automatic, far beyond *Nerka*'s control. There were other things to occupy the fish, above all the impossible tasks of migration.

Many believe the salmon cannot smell his stream far at sea although there are those who speak knowingly of varying salinity. Not everyone who ponders these things can bring himself to believe that even the salmon's incredible senses could provide for a chemical track through an ocean from one continent's environs to another. The sun then?

SOCKEYE

Perhaps. Some so believe. *Nerka* left his original continent behind with the sun striking the water at an angle; the rays of that sun could refract, reflect and penetrate the upper layers of the ocean at least in a way to distinguish that angle. Could the salmon absorb that imprint, too? But in those latitudes there is thick fog at least 25 per cent of the time. Yet, some do believe in the sun and the way it speaks to the salmon headed to sea, and that the salmon can reverse that mark upon its primitive brain and track it back at least to the vast reaches of the complex estuary. If it is not the sun, what then? If we believe in the salmon, must we also believe in the theory of the sun and the way they are linked in this miraculous happening? Some say it is the moon and who is to know they are wrong?

Nerka turned toward North America. In the sea he could make that orientation. He ignored Central America, South America and Mexico. He denied the route of the gray whale and the bill fish, he ignored Baja California and the vast coast of California itself. He scanned and passed and left behind the coasts of Oregon and Washington and the province of British Columbia. Pivoting in the sea, rising, charged with chemical signals, he chose a direction. He ran across currents and the sweeping arms of vortices. Spirals in the sea were items to cross as, like a hand on a giant clock, he swept across thousands of miles of coast and started forward. He began beating his way toward the soft, warm underside of Alaska. There was the sun. It fell ninety-three million miles through a largely hollow sky and perhaps spoke to this single salmon. If this is true, *Nerka*, alone since birth, since hatching, was mated to the sun and was alone no more. Brother to the sun, he would be seen home to where his nose and sense of taste could take over and berth him like a liner in from the ocean.

SOCKEYE

This animal who had never felt an emotion, who had never had a thought, who had never reasoned a move or wanted one thing more than another in a conscious way, this cold-blooded, tough and tried veteran of lonely years would be by this theory linked now to the heat of his sister the sun. If that is not a miracle and if that is not of a grander design, then no miracle can ever be defined and no design will ever exist.

But what of those who say that the salmon's response to his migratory cue is inherited and not memorized in any way? They say that navigational ability is solely an inherited response to environmental stimuli, that the circuits of a salmon's years are planted deep inside, imprinted upon its chromosomes. Again, we wonder, implant of inheritance, sun, salinity, the moon—some of these, all of these, none of these, many or all in a sequence? Perhaps a salmon ripples through one response sequence after another and while we seek the one the fish uses all. This thought is no better or worse than any other.

But there is yet another idea and this one seemingly almost mystical—yet not really so. Men ponder electrical stimuli. We do not know all that a salmon receives from the sea. Could it be this? They say that infinitely small voltages are generated as ocean currents travel through the earth's magnetic field. They speak of signals trickling through the sea that man cannot detect yet that could perhaps reach the fish through his lateral lines. Possibly the fish, like a plane on instrument approach, seeks the one and true glide path to destiny. Is the homing fish locked to an ultimate and original place by what to us is unmeasurably but to it is finite, perfect and unreleasing?

We know little of magnetism, gravity, electrical fields, of tiny voltages, and we must not turn away and say *no*, for to do this would be to miss the point and the value of our ignorance. If we deny our ignorance, we could question the value of the salmon, for what value lies in a teacher if the student knows all? We turn to the salmon since in the miracles of its life our lessons lie and one of them, surely, is humility.

By one or some or all of these things, by salinity gradients and microcosmic shifts, by hot sun or cool moon, by memory or measurement, by imprint or recall, by electricity and magnetism, by means so profound we must perhaps forever wonder, *Nerka* chose his course. He was going home to claim his immortality and die. Whatever means he used to accomplish all of this, that ability would be repeated again when his sperm met the hen's eggs, and whatever it was that came to him would then go to those that would follow. Whether *his* success as a salmon would help ensure theirs, whether a single generation in eternity imprints on a kind is not known—only that a thousand and a million generations do. The marvel is that none of these things mattered to *Nerka* continent-bound and only we, the *Nerka* watchers, could wonder or care or feel the frustration of not knowing.

Chapter

19

The color changes *Nerka* was to undergo had not yet been more than hinted at. His sleek silver coinage sides were darkening slightly, but the hot flush of carmine red would not appear until he reached sweet water. The changes in his head and face had started, though, and the hump on his back had begun to form. The female he was destined to encounter in the upper reaches of the Coppertree, Coppertree Creek above the lake, would be duller in color and have nowhere near the fierce mien that would mark him as a male. She, too, was in the sea and she too was pushing for home. She had been to sea one full year longer than *Nerka* and was fat and full of potential.

Nerka was fully mature, he was two feet nine inches in length and weighed more than the average of his kind—he was only a little short of nine pounds. Five to seven would have been average for him, although some few sockeye do reach the massive bulk of fifteen pounds. They are rare, however, and at his weight of eight plus pounds *Nerka* was a kind of giant. His fins were intact despite his years in the sea, and there was little fraying. That would come in the river. He pushed along hard much of each day, jetting water back from under his gill covers forty times a minute. The water flowed along his side and kept the sea that pushed in against him on all sides from forming turbulent circular currents. Such currents create drag and drag tires a fish and makes it use up fat. If *Nerka* arrived at the foot of his stream depleted, he would be likely to fail his final test. Only the fullest of the returnees, only the strongest and the fittest finish the trip. A fish is built in the sea, not worn, and if a fish survives the sea by chance alone and not by the power it has found in growth and maturity, there is one final culling. No salmon species can tolerate anything but the very best there is at the end of the sea journey. Everything a salmon does during its lifetime is designed at least in part to protect those last few minutes from anything but perfection.

And the mathematics of it? How do salmon numbers fare? *Nerka* had been one of just over 3600 fertile eggs that had been placed in the gravel by his mother and father— her eggs and his milt combined. Of the 3600, 106 smolt had made it through the lake and as far as the sea. Of those 106, ten survived to reach the mouth of the Coppertree system again. But there was the final test, for of those ten eight would die in their attempts to move upstream. Two of the more than 3600 eggs of which *Nerka* had been a part would reach their natal bed again and spawn. Two out of over 3600, less than one-tenth of 1 per cent, but what a tenth that is! Chance, yes, had played its part, but only perfection could have played off chance like a backboard and the two that would live to spawn were perfect in all respects. Thus the salmon living as an individual knows a life of constant hazard and survives as a species strong and full and ripe with the future. The two that survived were the perfect number for salmon survival and the salmon's environment would not be strained.

Nerka began to sense the faintest strains of sweet water memories as he approached the coast and turned north into Cook Inlet. The water grew less salty and more noisy with each mile. There were boats overhead in great numbers and the sloping floor of the sea had more to do with the surf and the tide than the ocean to which he had long since accommodated himself. Things rattled against each other with every surge, and the hissing sand and tinkling debris of rock and shell and human jetsam hummed into the water and filled it with sensations missing in the relative quiet of deep water far from the coast.

In the stream above Coppertree Lake and in the lake itself chemicals leached into the water, drained from fissured rock and pockets trapped in the earth by glaciers, quake and crust shove. No square foot of earth is absolutely identical to any other, no creek bed, certainly, and no lake floor. The chemicals that fed into the water in the system *Nerka* sought were distinct and were a part of his chemical memory. How much of that memory he acquired as an infant fish and how much came printed on his chromosomes has never been deduced, but it was a functioning memory as he approached the shore of the inlet where he would have to turn away from the sea forever. He tasted his way along, sampling finger after finger of freshwater that intruded upon the still essentially saline world. He fed in the inlet for three final days. He ate small fish, some copepods although they were small fare now, and he found a half-dismembered crab in a sloping area that promised and then forgot a false beach. He pulled at it and then turned west again to coast the roof of the inlet. He came to an area that arrested him and swam several times in a tight circle. He came out of his pattern at last and turned north. He began pushing against cold, clear saltless water that pulsed down toward him from higher ground. He tasted it and although he was without knowledge of the event inside his brain, small segments began to slip together. Small response patterns began to move into position. His taste was true and he had arrived at the foot of his final test. The crab he had helped pull apart on the sloping, rubble-strewn sand of the inlet only slightly farther east was to have been his last meal. He would never eat again no matter how tempted, no matter what was offered. He was fat, full of strength, ready. The carmine was deepening by the hour. His tail and head were deepening away from silver, too, in the direction of the other end of the spectrum. They were pea green and contrasted handsomely with his now slat-sided body flushed and ready. His muscle meat, too, had deepened in color and oxygen absorption and transport were at maximum efficiency. *Nerka* was ready for the test that was to follow, for this was the beginning of his spawning run.

Chapter

20

The timing of the salmon run is not a secret, and other
creatures build a period of their lives around the excitement of this annual event. They gather and deepen the
hazards of the test. Sea sharks cruised along just below the
surface dropping down on clusters of salmon pushing hard
toward their fate. Some salmon are culled there.

In the inlet and in the early river reaches men in boats
and along the banks set traps and cast lines and take their
toll. Eagle and osprey wing above and hold in tight ascending spirals of spring-heated air. Spotting salmon they
drop, swinging their feet forward at water touch, and many
struggle away with a salmon they are barely able to lift.
Salmon still alive are pulled apart and consumed strip
after strip. *Nerka* held deep and did not attract the birds'
talons, but the river was narrowing and the floor was
climbing closer.

In the narrow places, and they came often once the estuary was behind, *Nerka* had to push himself against and
through rushing water that tried to return him to the sea.
As though ascending stairs, he climbed from pool to pool,

often in the face of water thundering down on top of him.
One pool was harder, even, than the others, and six times
he was driven back, pushed down and beyond the rocks.
He circled in a small back eddy away from the rush of the
main stream and equalized his body chemistry. Once settled he again turned into the stream and aimed himself at
his destiny. Arching with all his strength, thrusting with
his tail and squirting water out from under his gill covers,
he drove hard again. He pushed by other salmon, males
and females, he slithered across them and passed others
that were failing for the last time. They were falling back
downstream and would be fished out by fox and bird and
other cullers as they came up against quieter banks below.
Nerka drove beyond them, over them, through their mass
and reached again the foot of the small tight place where
the flow was compressed between two high-standing
rocks. He thrust one last time, with all of his strength, and
he cleared the top, leaping out of the water to accomplish
it. He fell back into a pool and drove hard to avoid being
swept back over again. He circled behind a rock to where
a small branch of the rushing stream whirled endlessly
and where he would be free of the current's main tug. He
pushed in hard against other salmon who sought that
safety too and no sooner found his place in the three-foot-
deep water than a mighty intrusion came through the surface above.

Beside the pool to which *Nerka* had retreated there was
a sandbar and earlier that day its possession had been
argued over and a determination had been made. A small
chocolate brown bear had contested the rights of a larger
bear and she, a sow barren and without cub although massive in size, had driven the young bear away. But then a
larger bear yet had arrived. His paws were fifteen inches

across and his weight was well past nine hundred pounds. He was golden copper on a base of raw brown sugar in color. He had driven the sow away and now he possessed the bar overlooking the pool. He fed all day and the beach he owned was strewn with the waste of salmon partly eaten. Fox scampered in the undergrowth and stole what they could, and ravens and magpies, ruder than any other creatures there, took their share and complained all the while. Mink moved along the bank as well and stole carcasses larger than themselves, and bald eagles sat about in trees turning their disdainful pale heads from side to side. Gulls were the noisiest; they hopped up and down, took off and landed and defecated often, often enough to make it seem more a gesture than a physiological necessity.

But the mighty bear was king there and the others fed upon his leavings only at his pleasure. Cranky always, he was nervous now, for there were bigger bears than he in the woods and they might at any time claim what he held to be his own. It wasn't his, of course, just something held by strength for a time.

It was the head of this mighty bear that exploded through the water almost directly above *Nerka*. *Nerka* squirmed sideways as the bear's head appeared, and the fish next to *Nerka* was taken. Those who love their bears fictional rather than true have the mighty ursines flipping their fish out onto the bank with deft swipes of a giant paw. The paw is there all right, but is only occasionally used and that to pin a fish to the bottom. Bears bite their fish and carry the flopping creatures up to higher ground in their jaws.

The bear grasped the dog salmon next to *Nerka* and a career as noble in the sea as *Nerka*'s was ended there. If the salmon dealt with fairness, the death of this salmon after so much struggle would have been unfair indeed. That is not, however, how the salmon thinks for he does not think at all. It was, perhaps, in our estimate *too bad,* but nothing more than that. Even the salmon taken by the bear was not sad, just eaten. As for *Nerka,* the call had been close but he was not *glad to be alive.* He was simply alive, still driven by the progress of his ripening, and he had other ladders to climb.

Nerka held back in the pool for several hours, for his exertions had tired him and he had adjusting to do. Several more salmon were taken from the pool, but each time *Nerka* escaped as did most of the others. At last he felt the equalization that meant he could tolerate further exertion and he pushed out of the pool and felt the rush of the descending river. He turned upstream and arching, flexing and driving with his tail, helped as much as possible by jets from beneath big opercula, he drove against the current again. Pool by pool, through rapid after rapid he pushed. How much harder it was than coming down had been.

In pool after pool he rested, the length of time depending on how difficult the last ascent had been. Sometimes he held for minutes only and in other places for hours. In one pool, after a ferocious battle with a spill that fell full seven feet, *Nerka* rested for a day. It had taken him eleven leaping assaults before he cleared the spill, and he was nearly dead by the time he found a back eddy and a pool. Bears hunted there, too, but again he was lucky, he was crimson red and conspicuous and his now black-speckled fins were frayed from the battering he had been taking. He was losing fat rapidly and his store of strength was being depleted by the hour. Yet each of those hours drew him closer to the last rapid below the lake and from there the ascent would be very much easier. But first he had to reach that lake where he could safely rest in deep, quiet water before the final push out and up to the stream where his egg had hatched and his life begun.

The bears that fed along the way and threatened *Nerka* in every pool he chose were cross giants that lived alone much of the time. Cannibals at times, and collectors of berries and carrion and beach flotsam, they gathered every year along traditional shallow streams and after arguing among themselves took favored spots each according to the degree to which it could bully its fellows. More than one bear died each year from the battering it took from its elders who demanded the better fishing spots. Distrustful and angry much of the time, they pushed each other away and claimed the easiest salmon on which they gorged themselves.

The bear and the salmon evolved in the same world, the bear culling and perhaps perfecting the salmon and the salmon feeding the bears. What this interplay really has meant in the betterment, perhaps the perfection of each or both, cannot be reckoned. It is true and known that the bears come each year to where the salmon run and as in some lethal fraternity hazing, the salmon must run the bear gamut. What the sharks and the barracuda and the *Orca* are in the sea, the brown giants are by the ascending stream. *Nerka* experienced close bear threats on a score of occasions but each time wiggled and writhed away across the backs of other salmon and through their midst by shove and convulsive drive. In shallow water, packed together with others in a badly needed quiet eddy, a salmon is a vulnerable thing, *Nerka* no less than the rest. Yet this hazard, too, he survived and perhaps that would be another skill he would impart in his egg-seeking milt once even the Coppertree Lake was behind and only the gravel beds remained.

Nerka spent days in his climb toward his fate. He was in almost constant bodily contact with hundreds, thousands of his kind but was no more a part of them now than he had ever been before. A brushing fish on an identical errand was a coincidence, and *Nerka* felt no sense of sharing. That was far beyond him. He was part of a climbing flood of salmon, and males and females alike were together but apart. The males had no use for the females yet, for the water was not right. As the tide of red-and-olive fish approached the upper reaches of the lower stream, though, some few did feed away into side streams, into small places under low-hanging branches. These were the smaller percentage of the fish that had been spawned there, and their incredible sense of smell told them when to single themselves apart. They found their gravel beds, below the lake, and began performing the rites most of the salmon would perform beyond the lake. Each fish sought a special place and bit by bit those that survived began to thin out. *Nerka* pushed on, for the lake was ahead and he could taste it. It was there and it waited and would accept him and offer less hazard than he had known in years. He pushed hard for the final goal before the gravel bed—and there it was. Suddenly the stream deepened and the taste of the lake was rich and full. The stream widened, too, and the current slowed accordingly. *Nerka* pushed forward and came to some reeds. There was depth and a new silence. He pushed forward again and the world expanded. Other salmon circled nearby seeking new orientation. *Nerka* pushed through their numbers, brushed by them and beyond. He sank toward the bottom and rested. For the first time in scores of hours he was not fighting a current and there were no bears near. No fish large enough to threaten him was to be found. For the first time in years he was safe and he could rebuild for the final drive, the final hazard of his spawning run. *Nerka* sank and rested and tasted the lake again. It was a brief respite.

Chapter

21

Nerka circled slowly in the lake and although he would not feed, he was rebuilding in another way. No other freshwater fish but the salmon could push through the sea for thirty or forty miles every twenty-four hours and then, without feeding, push eighty miles up a descending stream against torrents and waterfalls, rapids and bears. It is hard for us to even imagine such exertions. No human athlete unaided could leap the leaps *Nerka* was forced to make at the foot of a score of spills. His task had been, by all reckoning, impossible, but it had been done nonetheless. He was bringing true salmon substance to the redd above the Coppertree. His milt would be the perfect stuff of salmon strength and skill.

Nature had no further use for her brush. *Nerka* shown brilliantly in the water. Near him other fish, too, had completed their color transformation—sleek males and egg-heavy hens, their sides distended with roe.

In the sea *Nerka* had accumulated parasitic sea lice and they probably slowed him down somewhat. Such hindrances would be fatal at the foot of a spill and a kind nature had worked a system through that was fair to all. In the sea the lice fed on *Nerka* and thrived. On the first taste of freshwater they began to die and fall away. By the time *Nerka* was half the distance to the lake, the last of the lice had drifted away. Other fish fed on them as they had once fed on a fish and *Nerka* was trim and neater for the battle ahead.

The ascent of the salmon is an exquisitely timed affair. The water must be right. Imperfect salmon who drifted off into side streams, confused because in the final test their senses had proven unequal to the enormous task, found overheated water and were struck by a deadly white furry moss—the fungus *Saprolegnia parasitica*. This disease of fish is fatal and no salmon in the red tide ascending would produce young once they sickened. In a very short time they would drift ashore, their sides barely heaving, and the fox, the otter and the birds would have them. In some small pockets in the stream underwater debris and chance produced too much nitrogen, and salmon lingering there were stricken with the bubble disease—first crippled and then killed by an effect rather like that which we call "bends" in human explorers of the sea.

Most of these hazards were avoided, though, because of the timing. The temperature of the water was right, the gas content with an exception was about right for the full length of the stressful run. The exception, of course, was oxygen, and the salmon had anticipated that and were at peak oxygen-use efficiency.

The salmon drifted in the lake as they had done when they were barely visible objects years earlier. Only now they did not feed and they did not hide. They held just off shore and circled quietly, a scarlet tide within the lake, full-humped, swollen and ready to be pugnacious. A few salmon had been born in the lake's shallows and they pushed off to those flattened areas and began their rituals. Magpies and ravens and crows walked in the inch-deep water on beds across which some salmon had to push in order to reach natal pools beyond. The squirming, struggling fish had their eyes pecked out and flopped grotesquely hollow-socketed and dying. The birds defecated and called and argued and threw themselves upon other defenseless fish. Eye after eye was stolen and fox rushed in among the squawking fury of pecking birds and dragged carcasses off for leisure eating.

Along the shores, too, there gathered an unusual assembly. Gulls up from the sea and some regular dwellers when the lakes were free of ice gathered and strutted in shallow water pecking at carcasses that floated some dead, some not quite dead. Among the strutting, arrogant gulls were others down from the wind. Wings tight against sleek strong body, long, finger-like primaries hidden in the general feather mass, there were eagles, cloud-dancers, sky-feelers, wind-lovers down among the gulls. Two hundred bald eagles picking for carrion like so many crows. Not ignominious, for the bald eagle is truly a scavenger when chance permits, and not unusual; although this species is rare in the forty-eight contiguous states, in places like Coppertree country they are still a common bird. So they came singly and in pairs to settle among the gulls, and the sky was empty without them. As strange a sight as that, two hundred noble sky warriors among the gulls seeking scraps and bits and leftover shreds of the salmon run.

The carnage continued. Every hour saw more salmon taken from the lake and its environs. The message had gone out in the land, and by that eternally mysterious means the news spread from species to species. Every predator and every scavenger that could gain from salmon flesh moved down to the lake and down to the streams, all staining deeper red each hour as the salmon pushed up from below, pushed beyond the opening from the sea, up the navigable river, up the streams, up over the spills and falls and torrents, over each other and in airborne leaps to reach this lake and stain it deeper and deeper with their flaring bodies.

Nerka began working his way toward an opening he knew was there, knew by the signals that came to him, the taste and the smell and the sub-aquatic ambience of natal place. He pushed through a stream of salmon coming against him, held back here and there by the crush of their bodies. Jammed together in the most intimate way they were yet apart by a universe, each pair, for they related as much to each other as the pebbles on a beach and with that much sense of self or belonging. Then he was beyond that tide and encountered another running across his front. It was there, in the midst of that lateral stream, that the smell was strongest, the texture of the water, its chemistry and temperature exactly right. This was the place he had lived his life to see again. He turned to his left and joined the flow. He pushed forward toward that one single outlet in the lake's northern shore that would bring him to the sacred redd. He pushed ahead reaching with his senses for the instant-by-instant reassurance that this was indeed, of all the streams in the world, the only right, real and correct stream for him. He would have no other chance, no other place, no other opportunity. If he was wrong, he would die and float backward in the current until taken up, dragged off and eaten, his milt still inside, his sperm still eager for the egg. *Nerka* was given this one last chance. All the things that he had been by promise as an egg, by promise as an alevin, a fry, a fingerling parr, as an adult fish in the sea, as an ascending red fury driven by himself, all of this came now to the final test. It was now and here alone. Once he left the lake he would either be right and reproduce himself and die, or simply die, a grim joke, a waste, an accident. But there was no irony that day. The sun was full and hard green needles of pine and the iridescent plumage of bird shone and kicked light, filling Coppertree with life. The waters were scarlet with urgent salmon of the sockeye kind. One of them, the one we have called *Nerka,* made his final selection. He was right, and he pushed out of the lake for the last time, rapidly approaching the place where his own egg had hatched so long ago down among the safe havens of the gravel. The water was right and *Nerka* pushed hard. His last imperative lay ahead. He would now accept the challenge and his ferocious mien made sense. With each minute he became more aggressive. For the first time in his life he related to other salmon in a direct one-to-one way. He was hostile to males—more hostile with each yard he covered—and was receptive to the sight and smell and taste of the females. In those last moments before he died, *Nerka* was not alone. He had bypassed sense of self, which he would never have, but he had reached a sense of others. Some he would seek and be attentive to, out of a necessity, true, but in a way we would like to anthropomorphize and call affection. That, for sure, would not exist in a salmon, but there is a salmon way of pairing that is unique enough to avoid chance hybridization.

Ahead, no more than yards ahead, was the miraculous goal. From the depths of the Pacific, from almost the shallows of coastal Asia, *Nerka* had come to within yards of the place where his journey had begun. Yards away and then only feet—he had done what was his to do as a descendant of the genus *Salmo. Nerka* descended, the perfect sockeye.

Chapter

22

It was the ritual time of mating and the river dance had begun. As *Nerka* approached a flat gravel area, the excitement in him built. Ahead a large ripe female rested. She had already begun her nest and was holding only momentarily before driving ahead with her labors. She was a full fish and prime, her tail and head were rich olive and her body was bright reddish-olive as were her fins. She was not quite as red as the males, as *Nerka* who approached her now, and her appearance was less pugnacious.

The female had chosen a perfect place. The water was twelve inches deep and the surface current eighteen inches per second, about the maximum the female would allow when she spawned, for her eggs must not be washed away. Deep in her nest, when it was completed, the current would be less than at the surface.

Nearby steely granite boulders appeared blue and the sun-drenched gravel had an ocher cast. *Nerka* nosed up close to where the female lay and prodded her once with his hooked and wicked snout. She turned away and continued her work. She rolled and turned in the current and the gravel that was displaced moved only slightly away, a little downstream. Her slow, strong undulations would continue for several days and nights until the redd was completed; a hollow place nearly ten inches deep was formed. There would have to be a flow of well-oxygenated water through the nest's eventual gravel cover and the current would have to be mild enough far down at the bottom so that egg and milt could survive.

While the female labored *Nerka* stood guard. He was angry now, for only constant outgoing anger could assure him of his place. Nearby other salmon leaped free of the shallow water, such was their excitement. They leaped for no apparent reason and flopped back and in. The battling males rolled over and over in a constant display of aggression, territorial claim and sexual prerogative.

The males outnumbered the females and this served to make them more ferocious yet, and, indeed, their ferocity, their aggression was like a final exam, a final test for the right to be immortal. Without books or buildings, art or style, without grave or name or recognition, what can a single salmon do to the eternity that is common for all species? Only by reproducing has a salmon truly lived at all.

While the female labored in the current to excavate their nest, *Nerka* faced off his rivals. With darting movements he pushed against and nosed into other fish who came too close. His movements were always tight and controlled, though, for he would rush back to stand again by the mate he had selected lest a third male arrive and usurp the place he had momentarily abandoned.

At times he had to fight, for other salmon were as large and determined as he. They would approach snapping their hooked jaws and formidable teeth in display. It was the ritual joust of the cock fish and at times it meant battle.

SOCKEYE

Nerka would be pushed so hard that he would charge the intruding male with bulldog-like temper and they would tumble and roll away in a brilliant red display amid quieter fish. Sides flashing as they tumbled, the two males would move away from the redd; *Nerka* would break off the contest as quickly as possible and rush back to protect that which he claimed. Sometimes the same opponent would return for another round, but mostly they drifted away and sought a female that had not yet been claimed or one taken by a lesser fish than *Nerka*. The river bottom quickly took on a pattern. Paired red salmon were everywhere and among them moved unattached males driven on by their own ripeness and by aggressive proddings from all sides. Only rarely did a fish manage to unseat an established male holding by a deepening redd.

Nerka held just downstream as the hen fish completed her work. Time and again she settled on the nest to test its depth with her ventral and anal fins. Each time she did *Nerka* would become excited and approach, but they were false starts, for she was not quite ready. Redds may vary in depth by as much as eight inches, from four to twelve inches. For this female, though, in this place ten inches were needed and she would not release her eggs until she had finished that task.

Finally she was done. She settled, tested the depth of her nest and rose slowly up above it. *Nerka* watched her carefully. She then sank down slowly until she nearly filled the hole she had excavated. She began working her jaws in a peculiar way; it would look to us as if she were gasping. *Nerka* knew, that information had come in his egg, and he moved over beside her. He, too, sank down into the nest. She shuddered once and her pale eggs began dropping into the opening below. *Nerka* also appeared to gasp and his orgasm occurred. His milt exploded out into the water and drifted down over the eggs. Sperm struggled, fully motile, and found their eggs. Some eggs drifted free and slipped over the downstream edge of the hollow. Smaller fish waited to gobble them up but 98 per cent of the eggs laid would be fertilized ten inches below the gravel stream bottom.

Their mating completed, the female rose and lifted free of the depression. *Nerka* followed suit but he held by the edge of the nest while the hen fish moved a few inches upstream. As they lifted clear, another male who had been nearby rushed across the nest and deposited his milt there as well. Then he was gone. *Nerka* was alert now only to fish that might try to eat the eggs that clustered and barely floated at the very bottom of the redd. The female began to roll as she had when she first started digging her nest. The gravel she dislodged tumbled downstream and filled her nest, covered her eggs. She kept at her new labors until six inches of selected gravel protected the eggs from predators, yet allowed them oxygen and enough current to free them of unwanted growths and chemical accumulations. That chore done, the hen fish turned again upstream. She would choose another place and begin again. In time she would accept another mate and go through the ritual for the second of four times before giving up and dying.

Nerka was alone again. The female was gone. Males no longer interested him as challenges and the place he had guarded so well was no longer of any concern. His milt had joined their eggs, his sperm had left him to continue him, and his few hours of relating to other specific creatures beyond the impersonal predator-prey arrangement were over. The female was gone and he, a ragged male, was of no more interest to other busy males than they to him. He turned away and lived, although his life was over, He moved slowly upstream but that had no meaning, and he turned downstream again. A hot, smaller cock fish darted at him but turned away quickly as if he realized that this male was spent and was gasping out a threatless denouement.

Perhaps if nature did not need the male to guard the eggs until the female can cover them the male could die the moment his orgasm was completed. But for this, and perhaps other reasons there is this period of life beyond life-giving. It is short and has no effect upon salmon kind. They are the hours between life and forever.

Nerka slipped farther downstream and ahead of him, at the westward bend in the Upper Coppertree Stream, the sun shot its rays at evening angle. The light entered before him and he blazed brilliantly red for those moments, his shadow cast long and black behind him in water only six inches deep as he drifted sidewise toward the bank of the stream, brilliantly red like a brief comet's history. And then the exquisite control he had had over his air bladder began to fail. Without knowledge of consciousness, *Nerka* began to lose it. His belly floated up. First he was on his side and he flopped his tail and then he drifted across rocks that rose up too far. He caught on them and continued to flop there until the sound he made attracted a fox. The small red and black dog of the forest floor slipped out from between two bushes and looked around. The sounds *Nerka* made flopping and gasping on the exposed gravel of the bank were too attractive to resist. The fox slipped forward in the failing light, he moved over to where *Nerka* lay helpless on his side. The fox looked down and then began to nuzzle the ragged, spent and dying fish.

GLOSSARY

ALEVIN Newly hatched salmon with the yolk sac unabsorbed.

AMPHIPOD A large order of Crustacea—about 4300 species now known. Most are marine. Includes sideswimmers, sand-hoppers, etc.

ANADROMOUS Describing fish that mature in salt water but return to fresh water to breed.

BIVALVE Having a hinged shell consisting of two parts instead of one, as in clam vs. snail.

BOSMINA A genus of freshwater Crustacea closely related to the water fleas.

CAROTINOID Any of several complex organic compounds imparting color to both plants and animals—most colors are derived from these compounds except green, white and black.

CILIA Short, hairlike structures capable of movement found in some types of animal cells.

CIRCULUS Also *sclerite*—a small ring-like marking on a fish's scale representing an increase in growth.

CLADOCERANS Fresh water crustaceans often found in vast numbers.

COELENTERATES The group of animals that includes hydroids, jellyfish, corals, anemones and related creatures.

COPEPOD Any of some 6300 known species of crustaceans in the subclass Copepoda.

CRUSTACEANS Any animal in eight classes of the phylum Arthropoda—included are water fleas, crayfish, crabs, lobsters, barnacles and many more. Composed of both marine and freshwater forms—over 30,000 species.

CYCLOPS Very common freshwater copepod.

DAPHNIA Very common cladoceran, often called *water flea*.

DENTICLE A toothlike projection on the scales of sharks and related primitive fish.

DIATOM Any of many forms of minute, unicellular or colonial algae—very primitive plant life.

EPISCHURA Fresh water copepods found in large, cold lakes.

FINGERLING An older juvenile Pacific salmon—between the *fry* and *smolt* stage. Atlantic salmon at this stage usually called *parr*.

FLUKE A horizontal portion of a whale's tail.

FRY Salmon young that have used up their yolk sac, have emerged from the gravel and are ready to feed.

GILL RAKERS A variety of projections and forms on the inner border of a fish's gill arch. May be wartlike, fingerlike or filamentous.

GYRE A circular or spiral motion; a body of water moving in such a fashion.

LIMNOLOGY The scientific study of lakes, ponds and streams and the life they contain.

LIPOID One of a group of fats and fat-like compounds found in living organisms.

MEDUSA BELL The bell-like part of a jellyfish.

MILT Mass of sperm suspended in fluid released by male fish.

MORPHOLOGY The form of a living organism considered as a whole.

OPERCULUM In fish, the gill cover.

ORGANOID Organ-like structure.

SOCKEYE

PARR The older juvenile, usually of the Atlantic salmon. The common equivalent in the Pacific species is *fingerling*.

PELAGIC Relating to open water in lakes and seas. Often used when water is over 60 feet deep.

PHOTOPHOBIC Repelled by light.

PHYTOPLANKTON All the microscopic plants suspended in an aquatic habitat—fungi, algae, etc.

PRIMARIES The outermost, principal flight feathers of birds.

REDD Spawning area of trout or salmon—often a circular depression in a gravel bottom.

SMOLT A young salmon ready to go to sea—used with both Atlantic and Pacific species.

TROPHIC SCALE The scale of who eats whom in the animal kingdom—the carnivores are at the top, the small plant-eaters at the bottom.

TUBULE A very small tube or tubular structure.

ZYGOTE A cell that results from the union of a male and a female gamete. (A gamete is a mature, functional sex cell—either egg or sperm—capable of joining with an opposite number to create a zygote.)